HOSPITALITY

GOD'S CALL
TO COMPASSION

PATTY
PELL

9 STUDIES
FOR INDIVIDUALS
OR GROUPS

T0339035

Life
Builder
Study

INTER-VARSITY PRESS
36 Causton Street, London SW1P 4ST, England
Email: ivp@ivpbooks.com
Website: www.ivpbooks.com

*Originally published in the United States of America in the LifeGuide® Bible Studies series
in 2008 by InterVarsity Press, Downers Grove, Illinois
First published in Great Britain in 2018*

British Library Cataloguing-in-Publication Data
A catalogue record for this book is available from the British Library

ISBN: 978–1–78359–684–3
eBook ISBN: 978–1–78359–685–0

Printed and bound in Great Britain by Ashford Colour Press Ltd, Gosport, Hampshire

*Inter-Varsity Press publishes Christian books that are true to the Bible and that communicate
the gospel, develop discipleship and strengthen the church for its mission in the world.*

*IVP originated within the Inter-Varsity Fellowship, now the Universities and Colleges Christian
Fellowship, a student movement connecting Christian Unions in universities and colleges
throughout Great Britain, and a member movement of the International Fellowship of
Evangelical Students. Website: www.uccf.org.uk. That historic association is maintained,
and all senior IVP staff and committee members subscribe to the UCCF Basis of Faith.*

Contents

Getting the Most Out of *Hospitality*

The word *hospitality* brings to mind tables filled with cookies and pots of good coffee. Being hospitable, in our understanding today, means to be gracious with your home and gifted at creating an atmosphere that invites community and relationship-building. Everyone appreciates this kind of hospitality, and it is an important aspect of serving others. However, biblical hospitality goes much deeper than plates of goodies, and it addresses the significant needs of the most vulnerable people.

Hospitality is one of the central characteristics of the nation of Israel in the Old Testament and of the kingdom of God in the New Testament. Hospitality, extended by the people of God to those outside the community, is to be a distinguishing feature of those who are in relationship with God. Hospitality is the extension of life to others, the meeting of needs and the provision of justice to those outside of the community, kinship or family. It is the outward-focused expression of the grace and provision that one has received from God.

This calling to extend life, provision and protection to others is around every corner in the Old Testament. Although there is no Hebrew equivalent for the word *hospitality,* the narratives, the Law, the Prophets and the Psalms are full of stories, commands and correctives that reminded Israel of their responsibility to those outside their own families. Many times these reminders were expressed in Israel's own identity as foreigners and aliens. Israel's great patriarchs saw themselves as aliens sojourning in a foreign land and in need of hospitality. This self-understanding was transferred to the whole nation of Israel in the time of oppression in Egypt. God delivered and provided for them, but he never let them forget that they were once vulnerable, oppressed and in need.

God exhorts his people to extend life, provision and protection to those around them who are the most vulnerable and most in need of special provision. For God's people this even meant sacrifice and suffering on behalf of guests as a response to God's deliverance in their own history. Hospitality in Israel ensured that family and kinship obligations did not eclipse the needs of others and, in turn, become corporate selfishness. Instead hospitality added to the depth of the family's experience and the community's relationships. The call was to provide for one's own kin, as well as those in need outside the familial structures. From Abraham to Moses to the kings and prophets, God's people were called to reflect God's character in their compassionate hospitality to all.

Jesus wrapped his ministry and teaching in the cloak of hospitality as a way of describing the kingdom of God. The extension of life, provision and protection was expanded as Jesus unpacked image after image of the kingdom of God in the language of host and guests. His parables and teaching reflect the openness, welcome and access that God the Father was now extending to all nations. Stories of banquets, feasts and parties flavor the ministry of Jesus throughout the Gospels. Some of his most significant teachings and miracles instruct his followers about who would be welcomed by the Father into the eternal banquet. Jesus played both the host with God the Father, as well as the guest needing to be invited into the hearts of his people.

Jesus' teachings hearken back to the obligations in the Old Testament of extending hospitality to those who are most vulnerable and in need. This understanding of hospitality continued to thread its way through the church's early history as people, who were once far apart, were united and found hospitality in Christ with one another.

It is this concept of ensuring that others outside ourselves or outside our own communities are cared for, protected and treated as family that distinguishes the church of Jesus Christ. Unfortunately, hospitality has been degraded into the "spiritual gift" of providing cookies for a church function when, in reality, it is to be one of the most important expressions of our faith. A true understanding of hospitality is a crucial corrective for many of us today, as we are in danger of degenerating into corporate church selfishness and leaving the most vulnerable in our society and world without the life, provision and protection that God has shown us.

The studies in this guide will lead you through both the Old Testament and the New Testament, where hospitality is described as a key characteristic of the people of God. The Old Testament studies cover a variety of genres—such as narrative, law codes, Psalms and the Prophets—in order to show that the kind of active compassion expected of Israel is found throughout its history and within every genre. The New Testament studies continue the same themes, beginning in the words and actions of Jesus in the Gospels and carrying through the period of the apostles. Hospitality is not limited to one historical period or one biblical writer, but it forms a thread that is found wherever you stop to look.

Suggestions for Individual Study

1. As you begin each study, pray that God will speak to you through his Word.

2. Read the introduction to the study and respond to the personal reflection question or exercise. This is designed to help you focus on God and on the theme of the study.

3. Each study deals with a particular passage so that you can delve into the author's meaning in that context. Read and reread the passage to be studied. The questions are written using the language of the New International Version, so you may wish to use that version of the Bible. The New Revised Standard Version is also recommended.

4. This is an inductive Bible study, designed to help you discover for yourself what Scripture is saying. The study includes three types of questions. *Observation* questions ask about the basic facts: who, what, when, where and how. *Interpretation* questions delve into the meaning of the passage. *Application* questions help you discover the implications of the text for growing in Christ. These three keys unlock the treasures of Scripture.

Write your answers to the questions in the spaces provided or in a personal journal. Writing can bring clarity and deeper understanding of yourself and of God's Word.

5. It might be good to have a Bible dictionary handy. Use it to look up any unfamiliar words, names or places.

6. Use the prayer suggestion to guide you in thanking God for what you have learned and to pray about the applications that have come to mind.

7. You may want to go on to the suggestion under "Now or Later," or you may want to use that idea for your next study.

Suggestions for Members of a Group Study

1. Come to the study prepared. Follow the suggestions for individual study mentioned above. You will find that careful preparation will greatly enrich your time spent in group discussion.

2. Be willing to participate in the discussion. The leader of your group will not be lecturing. Instead, he or she will be encouraging the members of the group to discuss what they have learned. The leader will be asking the questions that are found in this guide.

3. Stick to the topic being discussed. Your answers should be based on the verses which are the focus of the discussion and not on outside authorities such as commentaries or speakers. These studies focus on a particular passage of Scripture. Only rarely should you refer to other portions of the Bible. This allows for everyone to participate in in-depth study on equal ground.

4. Be sensitive to the other members of the group. Listen attentively when they describe what they have learned. You may be surprised by their insights! Each question assumes a variety of answers. Many questions do not have "right" answers, particularly questions that aim at meaning or application. Instead the questions push us to explore the passage more thoroughly.

When possible, link what you say to the comments of others. Also, be affirming whenever you can. This will encourage some of the more hesitant members of the group to participate.

5. Be careful not to dominate the discussion. We are sometimes so eager to express our thoughts that we leave too little opportunity for others to respond. By all means participate! But allow others to also.

6. Expect God to teach you through the passage being discussed and through the other members of the group. Pray that you will have an enjoyable and profitable time together, but also that as a result of the study you will find ways that you can take action individually and/or as a group.

7. Remember that anything said in the group is considered confidential and should not be discussed outside the group unless specific permission is given to do so.

8. If you are the group leader, you will find additional suggestions at the back of the guide.

1

Hosting the Traveler

Genesis 18:1-16;
Exodus 2:15-22

When we need to travel somewhere, we jump on a bus, a subway train or hop in our own personal vehicle. Traveling across the country does not usually include economic hardship or emotional distress. Often we choose to travel to vacation, experience new sights, or to visit friends and family. The idea of "travel" has positive and exciting connotations! Yet, in the ancient world, this was definitely not the case.

Travelers in the ancient world did not embark on their travels lightly. Traveling was usually prompted by the need to escape danger or economic hardship, such as drought. Imagine a traveler in the ancient world, dressed in robes, trying to avoid the heat. Imagine the fatigue, the lack of good food and water, and the fear of falling prey to robbers and other dangers. Imagine this traveler fleeing life-threatening circumstances, hoping to find sustenance and provision. Imagine this traveler journeying through foreign lands, unaware of the customs and ways of life of the surrounding people. This traveler is the kind of traveler encountered in the pages of Scripture, not the happy, expectant trekker of much of the modern world.

However, there are people in your community who may have

experiences more like those travelers in the ancient world. We may perceive these people as "strangers."

GROUP DISCUSSION. What individuals or groups in your community do you view as "strangers"?

PERSONAL REFLECTION. What has been your personal response to the individuals or groups you perceive to be strangers?

Abraham and Sarah met some unexpected travelers one day. *Read Genesis 18:1-16.*

1. What are all the things that Abraham, Sarah and the servants do to host the travelers in Genesis 18:1-16?

2. How is it costly to Abraham to serve the visitors in these ways?

3. What is Abraham's attitude toward the visitors in Genesis 18:1-16?

4. Think of a time when you had unannounced visitors. What was your attitude toward them?

How did you respond?

---

5. How might Abraham and Sarah feel when the travelers deliver their message (Genesis 18:9-16)?

---

6. What does the interaction between Sarah and the visitors reveal about her (Genesis 18:9-16)?

---

7. How are the roles of host and guest reversed throughout this story?

In Exodus 2, Moses, who has grown up in Pharaoh's court, sees a Hebrew being mistreated, and in the process of defending the Hebrew, Moses kills an Egyptian. *Read Exodus 2:15-22.*

8. How might Moses feel at the time he sits down at the well in Midian (Exodus 2:15)?

9. What are all the ways in which Reuel (later referred to as Jethro) extends hospitality to Moses (Exodus 2:18-22)?

What would it cost him to act in these ways?

10. How does Reuel cross ethnic boundaries in his hospitality to Moses?

11. The acts of hospitality in these two passages played a pivotal role in the plans of God. Because Abraham extended hospitality to the travelers, they came to be in his house to deliver the message of the covenant. In a similar way in Moses' story, it is because of hospitality that Moses was rescued from a dangerous situation. Moses lived in Midian for forty years, where he would experience many lessons that would be useful for his eventual role as deliverer. How is the way we treat people today potentially related to God's work in the world?

12. How can we cultivate attitudes of service, sacrifice and urgency toward ministering to others?

13. Think about the travelers and strangers in your community. What might it look like to extend hospitality to them in similar ways as Abraham and Reuel did?

Spend some time praying for the people in your community that you identified as "strangers." Pray for blessings in their lives. Pray for direction and courage to act in specific ways in order to extend hospitality to them.

Now or Later

Read the daily newspaper with an eye for hospitality this week. As you read through the news, think about what it would look like to extend hospitality to those mentioned in various news articles who are clearly in need. Discuss some of your thoughts with your group or with friends.

2

Loving Out
of Remembrance

**Deuteronomy
10:12-22; 24:10-22**

A few years ago, our family built a house. We did much of the labor ourselves, but we hired a general contractor to put up the frame of the house. Our contractor, in turn, hired various laborers to work for him. One day a man came to us and complained that he had not been paid by our contractor for the work he had done on our house. He had been waiting and had not received any of his hard-earned wages. As we tried to pin down our contractor on this oversight, we were given many justifications for the delay. But no matter what the administrative and bureaucratic reasons, this laborer continued to be without the finances to feed his family and pay his bills. Because of his low income, he had no credit on which to rely for the interim until he got paid, and he had no other means of providing for his family. To the contractor, it was a matter of "getting around to it," but to this laborer it was a matter of buying bread for each day. My husband and I wrote a check that day for the laborer.

Our actions reflect not only an understanding of others' needs and situations, but also our understanding of who God is.

GROUP DISCUSSION. Discuss the characteristics of God that you can think of and all the ways that he has shown you his grace.

PERSONAL REFLECTION. In what specific ways does your life reflect the character of God so much so that others notice it?

In Deuteronomy 10 God reminds the Israelites that they must reflect their history, God's grace to them and their specific mission to the world. These truths must all shine forth in the very specific daily actions of the Israelites. The church has the same call today. *Read Deuteronomy 10:12-22.*

1. How does Moses describe God's character and graciousness to Israel (10:12-16)?

2. What does Moses say should be Israel's response to God (10:12-16)?

3. Moses connects three groups in verse 18: the fatherless, the widow and the alien. Why do these groups in particular need God's grace?

4. Moses reminds Israel of their time of slavery and oppression in Egypt. What is his purpose in calling them to remember this experience (10:19-20)?

---

5. Try to recall a time in your life when you were in need. How has that experience changed you?

How might God want you to respond to that time in your life?

We turn now to Deuteronomy 24. This passage is in the midst of one of the main law codes of the Old Testament and this particular section is filled with laws describing how people should respond and react to others. The law codes stem from Exodus 19:3-6, which is in essence, a mission statement for the nation of Israel, calling Israel to be a witness to the nations around them. They are to do this by being a "holy nation," living differently from their neighbors in ways that will appeal to others and draw them to Yahweh. The law codes then describe the ways in which Israel should live, ways that would reflect the heart and character of God. *Read Deuteronomy 24:10-22.*

---

6. What are the circumstances of all the groups of people that are mentioned in Deuteronomy 24:10-18?

7. What is God particularly concerned about in these verses?

---

8. These laws contain motivational clauses or clauses that give the reason for obedience. What does the text in Deuteronomy 24:10-18 say should motivate the Israelites to obey these laws?

---

9. What is God's intent in the "gleaning laws" in 24:19-22?

---

10. What will it cost the Israelites to live in obedience to the laws in these verses (24:10-22)? Put another way, how will certain Israelites benefit from not following these laws?

---

11. What is the relationship between God's grace and the commands of God in these two passages of Deuteronomy?

---

12. What does hospitality look like in these two passages?

13. Where might you be benefiting from a system that takes advantage of the most vulnerable people?

---

14. How have you experienced God's grace in the life of your community?

How can your communal life reflect this grace through the treatment of the most vulnerable people around you?

Question 13 helped to identify areas of life where you might be benefiting from others' misfortune. Ask God to speak to you about this area of your life. Sit in silence, listening for the words that God has for you regarding your attitudes or actions. Spend a few moments praying together as a group about what God may have said.

Now or Later

Commit to having a conversation with someone who comes from another country but is residing in your community. Ask this person about his/her experience in your community. Ask about the things that have been difficult and the needs that he/she has had. Listen. Listen. Listen.

Rent the documentary *The Lost Boys from Sudan* and follow that with a discussion related to the themes of this study.

3

Kindness Beyond Expectations

Ruth 2; 4:13-22

In our community, there is a large group of resettled refugees from an African nation. They have come without many members of their families, and they are trying to adjust to life in the United States and life in a very cold climate. One of the places where some of them have found work is at the local Wal-Mart. There used to be a bus stop there. Budget cuts and other logistical details were addressed by city officials by canceling the bus route that ran from the Wal-Mart neighborhood to the side of town that houses many of the area's laborers and Wal-Mart employees. Consequently, employees now are faced with decreased safety, brutal weather and decreased social connections, as they are forced to walk through town or find other employment.

Sometimes the decisions we make do not take into account the most vulnerable among us. Some decisions or actions may be rational and logical. They may make financial sense or even be the "most that one can expect." But there are those among us that need more than what is expected.

GROUP DISCUSSION. What are the normal expectations of hospitality in your church?

PERSONAL REFLECTION. When in your life have you been in a situation where you felt like these African refugees? Think about a time when you needed hospitality and no one seemed to see or understand your need.

The book of Ruth begins with the story of Naomi, an Israelite, who finds herself in Moab with her husband and two sons, due to a famine in Israel. Over the course of time, Naomi's sons marry, and her husband and sons die, leaving Naomi with two daughters-in-law. Naomi begins the journey home to Israel and urges her two daughters-in-law to stay in their own land. Orpah stays in Moab, but Ruth, in an act of hospitality, returns to Israel with Naomi. These two husbandless women face a difficult life in Israel. Ruth is a foreigner, and both are poverty-stricken and without aid in a context where husbandless women are extremely vulnerable. *Read Ruth 2.*

---

1. What do you learn in 2:1-3 about the characters, Ruth and Boaz, and their situations?

---

2. How would you feel in Ruth's situation?

3. How do the harvesters view Ruth (2:4-7)?

---

4. Note all the ways that Boaz cares for Ruth in 2:8-16. How does Boaz go above and beyond what is expected of him?

---

5. What kinds of things would people say about your own character?

---

6. How does Ruth respond to the generosity of Boaz throughout 2:8-16?

---

7. In 2:17-23, Ruth and Naomi respond to the actions of Boaz. How do they feel about him?

---

8. How does the hospitality of Boaz make a difference in the lives of Ruth and Naomi?

9. *Read Ruth 4:13-22.* How does the hospitality of Boaz affect the history of Israel and God's plan for the world?

---

10. Boaz provided protection, provision and blessing to a foreigner. Think of a person in your life in a similar situation as Ruth. How can you go above and beyond what is expected to extend this kind of hospitality?

---

11. What is one thing that you can incorporate into your daily life to help you remember the person who you identified in question 10?

Spend a few moments praying for the person in your life who is in a situation like Ruth. Pray for God's provision and blessings in material and spiritual ways.

Now or Later

Take some time this week to find out if there are immigrants with specific needs in your community or if there are resettled refugees within your town/city. Spend some time praying for them and asking God to fill you with compassion and empathy for their situations.

4

A Heart
of Hospitality

Psalm 146

I opened the package that had arrived in the mail and found
the novel that I had been wanting for several months. My good
friend, Bob, had taken the time to find it, package it and send
it in the mail to me. It was one more example of his care and
compassion for me. Yet Bob is not only this way with me, he
responds to everyone in his life in a similar fashion. Bob's life
is characterized by concern for others, kindness, humility and
empathy. It is because of these qualities that I turn to him for
advice and direction. I can easily trust his advice and allow him
access to my life because I am confident of his character.

GROUP DISCUSSION. In your community what are the things,
people or places that people put their trust in or hope on?

PERSONAL REFLECTION. Where are you tempted to place your
trust or hope instead of in the Lord?

It is because of God's unchanging character that we can approach him and find a trustworthy place for our faith. *Read Psalm 146.*

---

1. Read Psalm 146 two or three times aloud. What feelings or impressions stay with you from the psalm?

---

2. Note how the psalmist begins his psalm (vv. 1-2). Why might he begin this way?

---

3. What is the psalmist contrasting in this entire psalm?

---

4. As a Christian, how do you find yourself putting your trust in "princes" and "mortal men"?

---

5. The psalmist exhorts readers to place their trust in the God of Jacob, their ancestor. Then he goes on to describe the characteristics of their God. What are the characteristics of God the psalmist focuses on (vv. 5-10)?

6. Which characteristic of God in these verses connects with your heart right now (vv. 5-10)?

7. In verses 5-6, God is portrayed in his role as the Creator God. How does it help us to trust in God by knowing that he is the Creator?

8. How do verses 7-9 exhibit the elements of hospitality that you have seen in previous studies?

9. If you were making the argument to trust in the Lord, which of God's character traits would you choose to emphasize?

How does it help us to trust in God by focusing on his characteristic of compassion for the vulnerable (vv. 6-10)?

10. How do the "righteous" (v. 8) and the "wicked" (v. 9) fit with the description of God's hospitable heart?

11. Many times we find ourselves in positions of weakness and vulnerability—physically, spiritually or emotionally. Where do you see yourself in this passage?

How do the words of this psalm speak to you?

---

12. Think of someone you know who is weak or vulnerable. Perhaps they are oppressed, discouraged, hungry, imprisoned or bowed down. How can you extend hospitality to them in ways that reflect the character of God from this psalm?

Break in to partners to pray, and spend a few minutes praying for one another about the areas where you feel weak or vulnerable. Pray the actual words of the psalm for one another.

Now or Later

Choose one of God's characteristics that is described in this psalm to focus on for the next week. Pray for a deeper understanding and experience of this characteristic during the week. Journal throughout the week about the times when you see this character quality displayed in your own life or in the lives of others. Pray that this quality would be increased in your own character.

5

Fasting the Lord's Way

Isaiah 58

As my family and several students walked through one of the Mulley Children's Homes in Kenya, I listened to the incredible story of the husband and wife who began this amazing place. Mr. and Mrs. Mulley sold all they had acquired through a very successful life of business in order to begin taking in street children and abandoned babies. Over the course of eighteen years, they built several children's homes; the one we were touring held over 800 children alone. The homes provide for the children in every way possible. They provide housing, education, health care, spiritual guidance and direction, physical activity, and friendships. They are incredible places of hospitality, taking in the most vulnerable members of society. And the spiritual benefits of extending this kind of hospitality are evident in the lives of the Mulley family and in the lives of the staff. Their spiritual lives are vibrant, deep and filled with rich dependence on the Lord. There is a clear and undeniable connection between the depth of faith and trust that this family has and their lives of extending hospitality.

GROUP DISCUSSION. How does your Christian community (church, small group, fellowship) seek out God?

PERSONAL REFLECTION. How do you try to keep the vitality in your relationship with God?

For me, the Mulley's orphanage reflects Isaiah 58:8: The light of their lives "break[s] forth like the dawn." *Read Isaiah 58.*

---

1. What are the initial emotions that are triggered for you after reading the whole passage?

---

2. What seems to be the purpose of a fast (vv. 1-3)?

---

3. What is the perspective of fasting that Israel has (vv. 3-5)?

---

4. There are four sections where God describes his perspective on fasting or seeking him. These sections are verse 6, verse 7, verses 9-10 and verse 13. What are the main characteristics of God's fast?

5. There are three corresponding sections that describe God's response to those who seek him according to his definition (vv. 8-9, vv. 10-12 and v. 14). What are the results of engaging in the Lord's kind of fast?

6. How would engaging in these activities and this kind of spirituality help an individual or a community to seek God?

7. Which of the actions depicted in verses 9-10 is most difficult for you?

8. Meditate for a moment on verses 6-7. What might these kinds of actions look like in your Christian community today?

9. Why does God use the images he does to describe what Israel will be like if they seek God in these ways?

---

10. How is the Lord's fast a description of hospitality?

---

11. How might you or your community change the way that you seek God?

Take some time to pray individually. Focus your prayers on repentance for the ways in which you and your community have "fasted" like Israel did, and for the ways you have ignored the needy.

Now or Later

Pick one aspect of the Lord's fast and make a plan to incorporate this into your life. Keep a journal of this discipline in order to see how your spiritual life changes.

Read through Amos 5. How does this chapter add to the knowledge and understanding you gained from this study?

6

Dwelling in Service

My daughter sat on the concrete floor at a Missionaries of Charity home in the Huruma neighborhood of Mathare Valley slum in Nairobi. She was painting the toenails of developmentally disabled women. She sang simple worship choruses to them as she painted, and then she would hold their hands and just sit with them. The room was filled with women, now all with brightly colored toes. I sat across the room from her, shelling peas and just watching. The words spoken by one of the nuns earlier in the day came back to me. The nun said that working at Huruma had shown her so much about Jesus. She gestured to the women in the room and passionately declared that caring for these women had shown her Jesus and had taught her more about him than any other experience in her life. As I sat and held the hand of one elderly woman and softly joined my daughter in a chorus, I wondered what that sister had meant. How had she seen Jesus? What was it she had learned?

GROUP DISCUSSION. When you think of the descriptors *righteous* and *cursed,* what comes to mind?

PERSONAL REFLECTION. For what reasons could Jesus call you "righteous" today?

Beginning in Matthew 21, Jesus is ministering in Jerusalem with his disciples. As Jesus and the disciples are leaving the temple (chapter 24), Jesus begins to discuss the events of the future and the attitude the disciples need to have as they wait for these future events. It is in this context that chapter 25 occurs, and it was this passage that came to my mind that day in the Nairobi slum. *Read Matthew 25:31-46.*

1. What is the setting of verses 31-33?

2. What responses or questions do you have as you read this text?

3. Scan the entire passage and find all the words or phrases that are direct contrasts. What is the passage contrasting?

4. Why do you think Jesus chooses the sheep and goats as the metaphor in this passage?

For what reason are the sheep and the goats judged?

---

5. What are the needs of the people described in verses 34-38, and how did the "sheep" meet those needs?

---

6. What is the connection between Jesus and the most vulnerable people?

---

7. Why are we tempted to ignore meeting the basic needs of people?

8. What is implied in the answer that the "goats" give in verses 41-45?

---

9. This is a difficult passage about the relationship between service and salvation. What makes this text so challenging for us?

---

10. Why is the presence of hospitality or the lack of hospitality worthy of the serious consequences described in this passage (v. 46)?

---

11. Jesus is talking to his disciples, thus making all the usages of *you* plural or corporate. What does it mean for your Christian community to live out the hospitality of the "sheep" corporately?

12. Think of someone that you know who has a very basic need. How can you meet this need this week?

Have one member of the group read verses 34-40 aloud. Read the passage two or three times while the groups sits in silence and listens. Each time the passage is read, listen for God's words to you. The final time the passage is read, listen for God's direction in your life. Spend a few minutes in individual prayer in response to what you sensed during the readings.

Now or Later

Find an article or book, such as a missionary biography, about someone who has spent his or her life ministering among the very needy. Or grab a cup of coffee with someone who ministers in this type of setting. Listen to their perspectives and their experiences of meeting Jesus. How does their life connect to Matthew 25:31-46?

7

Offering
Your Resources

Mark 6:30-44

It is a wonderful thing to see when people pull together, using their talents and passions to serve others. Pamba Toto is a jewelry business that was started in the United States by two women with a heart for orphans in Africa. One of the women is an incredible artist and expresses her passion through creating beautiful jewelry. She searches for interesting and unique beads all over the world and pours out her time and talent in order to place them into creative pieces. Her partner visits Africa every summer, visits the orphanage and searches for distinctive beads to bring home. At home in the United States, she spends her time and talent selling exquisite jewelry to her friends while she tells the story of these little ones who are loved by God.

Each of these women has been given resources. None of the talents or resources alone is spectacular or breathtaking. It is the vision of these women and what they do together that makes all the difference.

GROUP DISCUSSION. Take five minutes to just list off all the needs that you can think of in your community and in the world.

What is your reaction to the list?

PERSONAL REFLECTION. Spend a few minutes writing out your thanks to God for all the resources, talents and blessings that God has given you.

In Mark 6, Jesus gathers his disciples to him, offers a few instructions, gives them his own authority and sends them out two by two. The disciples preach repentance, drive out demons and heal the sick before they gather together once again with Jesus. *Read Mark 6:30-44.*

---

1. Try to put yourself in the shoes of the disciples. What are the emotions and needs that you might be experiencing when you gather together again with each other and with Jesus?

---

2. How might the disciples feel about the crowds?

---

3. What is the conflict that is emerging in this passage (vv. 30-34)?

4. What prompts the compassion of Jesus in this passage (vv. 32-34)?

_____

5. Who are the people or the specific needs of people that you wish you could just "send away"?

_____

6. What are all the obstacles that the disciples face in giving something to eat to the crowds?

_____

7. When you think of all the needs of the world, what are the obstacles in meeting some of those needs?

_____

8. How does the miracle of feeding the crowds take place (vv. 38-44)?

9. Jesus took the resources of the people and the disciples and used those very resources to meet the needs of the crowds. What does it mean for you or your Christian community to offer your resources to Jesus so that he can meet the needs of others?

10. What keeps you from offering your personal, financial, emotional and physical resources to Jesus?

11. What are your unique talents, spiritual gifts or passions that Jesus could use in order to meet the needs of others?

It is the power of Jesus that took the meager resources of the disciples and crowds, and used them to extend hospitality to all. Pray for the strength to offer up your resources and for the power of Jesus to use those resources to minister to others' needs.

Now or Later

Read Matthew 25:14-30. What does this passage teach about using the resouces that God has given?

8

Feasting Through Sacrifice

Luke 22:7-30

There is an island in the Hawaiian islands called Molokai. It was designated as a leper colony in 1866. All the lepers from all the other islands were rounded up, separated from family and friends, and exiled to Molokai for the remainder of their lives. Many of them did not even survive the boat trip, as they were tossed out of the boats into the churning water and rocky coastlands of the island. In 1873, a Catholic priest, Father Damien, came to the island. He exiled himself in order to care for the lepers. He nursed them, encouraged them, taught them and shared Jesus with them. Years later, the lepers on the island buried Father Damien. He had contracted leprosy and had become one of them, succumbing to the disease with his life. His sacrifice in order to minister to others had required of him the greatest sacrifice.

GROUP DISCUSSION. Think of someone you know who is a great host/hostess. What makes them so effective at hosting?

PERSONAL REFLECTION. Who has authority in the world today? How is authority used?

The greatest sacrifice in human history was the sacrifice Jesus made in his death on the cross, laying down his authority for all of humankind. The evening before his death, Jesus tried to explain the great truths about servanthood and sacrifice. *Read Luke 22:7-30.*

---

1. List all the references to eating and drinking in this passage.

---

2. What images and emotions come to mind when you think of eating and drinking?

---

3. How is Jesus the guest in verses 7-13?

---

4. What are all the ways during the meal in which Jesus connects his life to the history of Israel?

5. How do ordinary items become symbols of hospitality in verses 14-20?

6. In what ways is Jesus the ultimate host in verses 14-20?

7. Describe how Jesus has been a host to you in your life.

8. What makes the disciples' argument so offensive in verses 24-30?

9. How do the Gentiles in verse 25 handle authority? What does this look like?

10. In verses 26-28, how does Jesus contrast his followers with Gentiles?

11. In what ways do you see Jesus using his authority in this passage?

12. How should the sacrificial hospitality of Jesus change us?

13. What are some specific ways that you can show sacrificial hospitality?

In silence, ask God to reveal one step of sacrificial hospitality that you can take this week. Pray about this step with one other person.

Now or Later

Study the other accounts of the Last Supper, particularly in John 13. How does the washing of the disciples' feet add to your understanding of the concepts of authority, service and hospitality?

9

Destroying Barriers

Acts 10

One of the most vivid pictures of heaven I have seen was at a conference for Christian college students. There were several ethnic groups represented, including Asian American, African American, Southeast Asian, Latino and Anglo students. One of the nights of the conference was a night of celebration and barrier-breaking. Each fellowship extended hospitality to the others by providing food and music from their cultural background. The night was then filled with the smells and sounds of the world. As the night progressed, students began to teach each other their own specific ways of dancing and praising the Lord. There were Asian students learning how to "stomp" and Latino students being tutored in the Indian dances of the Southeast Asian students. The party went late into the night and, because of the simple hospitality of food, music and fellowship, barriers had begun to be broken.

GROUP DISCUSSION. Look through the daily newspaper and find examples of barriers between people. How does the existence of these barriers affect all of us?

PERSONAL REFLECTION. Describe a time when you felt you were trapped behind some kind of barrier or obstacle.

Although the story of the college conference is a picture of the kingdom of God, the early church did not find such reconciliation easy. Instead, the church wrestled with barriers and reconciliation as they struggled to understand the breadth of the gospel. Peter is one of the first apostles to come face to face with the destruction of a well-established barrier. *Read Acts 10.*

1. This story is about two individuals, Peter and Cornelius, and God's call to them both. Describe the characteristics and traits of Cornelius that are revealed throughout the entire passage.

2. What would have made this call difficult for both Peter and Cornelius?

3. Think of a barrier that exists between you and someone else—either in your neighborhood, church, school or community. How would that relationship be different if the barrier did not exist?

4. What are the similarities and differences between the visions Peter and Cornelius received?

5. In verses 9-16, Peter is faced with a strange vision of unclean animals with the instruction to eat them. What might the Lord be trying to communicate to Peter by asking him to do such an unnerving thing?

6. What barriers are being crossed in verses 22-26?

7. When have you had an experience of crossing a barrier or seeing a barrier crossed in your own community?

8. At this point in the narrative, Peter has come a very long way since his interaction with God during his vision. What does Peter learn and come to accept in verses 27-35?

9. In verses 34-43, Peter shares the gospel message with Cornelius's household. What are some surprising elements of the message about Jesus that Peter includes? Why does he include these?

10. In verses 44-48, what changes about the ministry of the church at this point in its development?

11. How does hospitality help break down barriers in this passage?

12. What is one action of hospitality that you can engage in with someone who is on the other side of a "barrier" from you? How can you cross a barrier or break down a barrier with this person?

Spend some time asking God for forgiveness for all the ways in which you, individually, and the church, corporately, have created or maintained barriers between people.

Now or Later

Study Ephesians 2:11-22. How does this passage inform your understanding of God's actions in history through Jesus?

Study John 4. How did Jesus break down barriers with the Samaritan woman?

Leader's Notes

MY GRACE IS SUFFICIENT FOR YOU. (2 COR 12:9)

Leading a Bible discussion can be an enjoyable and rewarding experience. But it can also be scary especially if you've never done it before. If this is your feeling, you're in good company. When God asked Moses to lead the Israelites out of Egypt, he replied, "O Lord, please send someone else to do it!" (Ex 4:13). It was the same with Solomon, Jeremiah and Timothy, but God helped these people in spite of their weaknesses, and he will help you as well.

You don't need to be an expert on the Bible or a trained teacher to lead a Bible discussion. The idea behind these inductive studies is that the leader guides group members to discover for themselves what the Bible has to say. This method of learning will allow group members to remember much more of what is said than a lecture would.

These studies are designed to be led easily. As a matter of fact, the flow of questions through the passage from observation to interpretation to application is so natural that you may feel that the studies lead themselves. This study guide is also flexible. You can use it with a variety of groups student, professional, neighborhood or church groups. Each study takes forty-five to sixty minutes in a group setting.

There are some important facts to know about group dynamics and encouraging discussion. The suggestions listed below should enable you to effectively and enjoyably fulfill your role as leader.

Preparing for the Study

1. Ask God to help you understand and apply the passage in your own life. Unless this happens, you will not be prepared to lead others. Pray too for the various members of the group. Ask God to open your hearts to the message of his Word and motivate you to action.

2. Read the introduction to the entire guide to get an overview of the entire book and the issues which will be explored.

3. As you begin each study, read and reread the assigned Bible passage to familiarize yourself with it.

4. This study guide is based on the New International Version of the Bible. It will help you and the group if you use this translation as the basis for your study and discussion.

5. Carefully work through each question in the study. Spend time in meditation and reflection as you consider how to respond.

6. Write your thoughts and responses in the space provided in the study guide. This will help you to express your understanding of the passage clearly.

7. It might help to have a Bible dictionary handy. Use it to look up any unfamiliar words, names or places. (For additional help on how to study a passage, see chapter five of *How to Lead a LifeBuilder Study*, IVP, 2018.)

8. Consider how you can apply the Scripture to your life. Remember that the group will follow your lead in responding to the studies. They will not go any deeper than you do.

9. Once you have finished your own study of the passage, familiarize yourself with the leader's notes for the study you are leading. These are designed to help you in several ways. First, they tell you the purpose the study guide author had in mind when writing the study. Take time to think through how the study questions work together to accomplish that purpose. Second, the notes provide you with additional background information or suggestions on group dynamics for various questions. This information can be useful when people have difficulty understanding or answering a question. Third, the leader's notes can alert you to potential problems you may encounter during the study.

10. If you wish to remind yourself of anything mentioned in the leader's notes, make a note to yourself below that question in the study.

Leading the Study

1. Begin the study on time. Open with prayer, asking God to help the group to understand and apply the passage.

2. Be sure that everyone in your group has a study guide. Encourage the group to prepare beforehand for each discussion by reading the introduction to the guide and by working through the questions in the study.

3. At the beginning of your first time together, explain that these studies are meant to be discussions, not lectures. Encourage the members of the group to participate. However, do not put pressure on those who may be hesitant to speak during the first few sessions. You may want to suggest the following guidelines to your group.

☐ Stick to the topic being discussed.

☐ Your responses should be based on the verses which are the focus of the discussion and not on outside authorities such as commentaries or speakers.

☐ These studies focus on a particular passage of Scripture. Only rarely should you refer to other portions of the Bible. This allows for everyone to participate in in-depth study on equal ground.

☐ Anything said in the group is considered confidential and will not be discussed outside the group unless specific permission is given to do so.

☐ We will listen attentively to each other and provide time for each person present to talk.

☐ We will pray for each other.

4. Have a group member read the introduction at the beginning of the discussion.

5. Every session begins with a group discussion question. The question or activity is meant to be used before the passage is read. The question introduces the theme of the study and encourages group members to begin to open up. Encourage as many members as possible to participate, and be ready to get the discussion going with your own response.

This section is designed to reveal where our thoughts or feelings need to be transformed by Scripture. That is why it is especially important not to read the passage before the discussion question is asked. The passage will tend to color the honest reactions people would otherwise give because they are, of course, supposed to think the way the Bible does.

You may want to supplement the group discussion question with an icebreaker to help people to get comfortable. See the community section of the *Small Group Starter Kit* (IVP, 1995) for more ideas.

You also might want to use the personal reflection question with your group. Either allow a time of silence for people to respond individually or discuss it together.

6. Have a group member (or members if the passage is long) read aloud the passage to be studied. Then give people several minutes to read the passage again silently so that they can take it all in.

7. Question 1 will generally be an overview question designed to briefly survey the passage. Encourage the group to look at the whole passage, but try to avoid getting sidetracked by questions or issues that will be addressed later in the study.

8. As you ask the questions, keep in mind that they are designed to be used just as they are written. You may simply read them aloud. Or you may prefer to express them in your own words.

There may be times when it is appropriate to deviate from the study guide. For example, a question may have already been answered. If so, move on to the next question. Or someone may raise an important question not covered in the guide. Take time to discuss it, but try to keep the group from going off on tangents.

9. Avoid answering your own questions. If necessary, repeat or re-phrase them until they are clearly understood. Or point out something you read in the leader's notes to clarify the context or meaning. An eager group quickly becomes passive and silent if they think the leader will do most of the talking.

10. Don't be afraid of silence. People may need time to think about the question before formulating their answers.

11. Don't be content with just one answer. Ask, "What do the rest of you think?" or "Anything else?" until several people have given answers to the question.

12. Acknowledge all contributions. Try to be affirming whenever possible. Never reject an answer. If it is clearly off-base, ask, "Which verse led you to that conclusion?" or again, "What do the rest of you think?"

13. Don't expect every answer to be addressed to you, even though this will probably happen at first. As group members become more at ease, they will begin to truly interact with each other. This is one sign of healthy discussion.

14. Don't be afraid of controversy. It can be very stimulating. If you don't resolve an issue completely, don't be frustrated. Move on and keep it in mind for later. A subsequent study may solve the problem.

15. Periodically summarize what the group has said about the passage. This helps to draw together the various ideas mentioned and gives continuity to the study. But don't preach.

16. At the end of the Bible discussion you may want to allow group members a time of quiet to work on an idea under "Now or Later." Then discuss what you experienced. Or you may want to encourage group

members to work on these ideas between meetings. Give an opportunity during the session for people to talk about what they are learning.

17. Conclude your time together with conversational prayer, adapting the prayer suggestion at the end of the study to your group. Ask for God's help in following through on the commitments you've made.

18. End on time.

Many more suggestions and helps are found in *How to Lead a LifeBuilder Study.*

Components of Small Groups

A healthy small group should do more than study the Bible. There are four components to consider as you structure your time together.

Nurture. Small groups help us to grow in our knowledge and love of God. Bible study is the key to making this happen and is the foundation of your small group.

Community. Small groups are a great place to develop deep friendships with other Christians. Allow time for informal interaction before and after each study. Plan activities and games that will help you get to know each other. Spend time having fun together going on a picnic or cooking dinner together.

Worship and prayer. Your study will be enhanced by spending time praising God together in prayer or song. Pray for each other's needs and keep track of how God is answering prayer in your group. Ask God to help you to apply what you are learning in your study.

Outreach. Reaching out to others can be a practical way of applying what you are learning, and it will keep your group from becoming self-focused. Host a series of evangelistic discussions for your friends or neighbors. Clean up the yard of an elderly friend. Serve at a soup kitchen together, or spend a day working in the community.

Many more suggestions and helps in each of these areas are found in the *Small Group Starter Kit.* You will also find information on building a small group. Reading through the starter kit will be worth your time.

Study 1. Hosting the Traveler. Genesis 18:1-16; Exodus 2:15-22.

Purpose: To understand that biblical hospitality is costly for the host, filled with sacrifice and deep service to those who are in need.

Group discussion. The opening question is designed to help the group truthfully evaluate their community and to truthfully identify the groups that are marginalized within that community. As a leader, gently challenge the group to think about those who are not perceived to be full members of their community. The group may identify individuals or groups, such as certain ethnic groups, groups with certain lifestyle practices or specific age groups. The goal of this question is to begin to help group members put themselves in the shoes of those in the community who are "strangers."

Personal reflection. Note that while these personal reflection questions are designed to be used by individuals studying on their own, it can also be a great follow-up to use in your group if time allows.

Question 1. This is an observation question that deals with the entire passage. Encourage the group to stay within the bounds of observation by stating all the actions of Abraham, Sarah and the servants. By reiterating all of these actions, the point of sacrificial hospitality will begin to be illuminated.

Abraham hurried to meet the travelers and bowed down, which was a sign of respect and service. The word *lord* (Gen 18:3) was used in the Old Testament as either a reference to God or as a general term used to designate respect for another person (it was often used by a wife to refer to her husband). Abraham provided water so they could wash their feet, and he hurried once again to enlist the help of Sarah and the servants. He selected a choice calf for the guests and the household, and provided a meal of the best meat, curds and milk. It is important for the group to identify that Abraham chose the best calf out of his herd. This will be instrumental in the following question. Notice also that Abraham stood while his guests ate their meal; this is another indication of the respect and honor given even to strangers in the ancient world.

Question 2. This question looks at the consequences of the previous question. To be hospitable in this story meant great sacrifice. Abraham willingly sacrificed his best calf in the herd, which may have caused economic consequences for his household later. Abraham, Sarah and the servants were willing to focus on the travelers and to spend the lengthy amount of time it would have taken to prepare such a meal.

Question 3. The attitude that Abraham had toward uninvited strangers and travelers is key to our understanding of hospitality. Help the group to look at the attitude that is revealed by the words of the story itself. The title *lord,* coupled with the request to serve the guests, shows that Abraham saw it as a privilege to serve. His repetition of the self-designation *servant* also reveals his attitude of hospitality (Gen 18:3, 5). He wanted to serve them, he fervently requested that they would not keep moving but allow him the pleasure of feeding and providing for them.

Question 4. The goal of this reflection question is to contrast the modern world's attitude toward guests. It is very important to distinguish the difference between various cultures in the modern world. There are some cultures, such as Western cultures, where the contrast between the Old Testament attitude and the modern attitude is acute. In other cultures, Old Testament-style hospitality is still expected and practiced. Depending on your group, this question can draw out the feelings that some may have of being imposed on by caring for guests and the tendency to view strangers as an interruption in the schedule. For other groups, this question may be more of a celebration, a time to acknowledge a positive attitude toward others. No matter what the composition of the group, it is important to highlight the kind of sacrificial hospitality that is shown by Abraham's household. It was costly economically as well as emotionally.

Question 5. Abraham and Sarah were extending the kind of hospitality that was integral to their culture and experience. People took great care to provide for travelers because they were usually in economic hardship or in danger. The travelers needed others to provide food and safety in order for them to survive. Abraham's household was extending this kind of service to strangers. The fact that these visitors brought a message from God to them specifically must have been quite a shock. The message was not new to Abraham and Sarah. It had been given and repeated (Gen 12; 15; 17) by God. Yet the promise of a son had not materialized.

It will be most helpful if the leader can help the group put themselves in the shoes of Abraham and Sarah. They had this promise, but they had not seen it happen. They did not expect these visitors to be messengers of God's word to them. They very well could have experienced surprise, doubt and anticipation.

Question 6. Sarah is skeptical that the message the travelers bring is ever going to come to reality. It is possible that Abraham had not shared with her the promise of an heir, and this could be the reason she laughed. However, this is unlikely. It is more likely that Abraham had not been able to convince her to trust in God's promise and that the reality of the present circumstances was too difficult to dismiss.

The interaction between the travelers and Sarah revealed her internal doubt and lack of faith. This is relevant to all of us, as we have doubt and unbelief that we never acknowledge or let others know about. Sarah laughed to herself out of this "secret" place of doubt. She was stunned when her internal lack of belief was made public. It may be that the very reason the travelers exposed her doubt was to bring it out into the open. This interaction was the occasion for the profound words of God's ability to do anything. This section of the story reminds us of God's great power in contrast to our weak faith.

This could be a great time in the study to further personalize the story by asking the group to think of a time when they had significant doubt about God's promises. As the leader, you may want to ask, "When have you experienced doubt about God's promises?" This may flow naturally from the study, but it could also feel too distant from the Genesis narrative. If this question is added, be sure to transition back into the narrative smoothly so that the flow of the study is not lost.

Question 7. In various biblical stories the guest and host roles are reversed. In this particular narrative, Abraham and Sarah begin as the hosts, providing nourishment and rest for the strangers that have come into their home. Yet, as the narrative continues, it is clear that the travelers bring a blessing to them as hosts. Abraham and Sarah are the recipients of a word from God and a blessing from these guests. The strict understanding of the host providing the blessing to the guests is altered as the hosts themselves become the guests in a sense. The "hosts" receive the ministry of the travelers. This role reversal will be seen in later studies and, in particular, in the New Testament passages.

Question 8. Moses' experience is exactly what many travelers in the ancient world experienced. He had fled his home due to danger; he fled into a foreign land. He was a stranger, who was unaware, perhaps, of the customs of the local people. He was weary from hard travel through inhospitable landscapes and was in need of food, water, protection and relationship.

It is crucial to this question and to the overall study that the group grasps how needy Moses was at this point in his life. He no longer had the societal structure needed to survive in the ancient world. He lacked family, support and any means of providing for himself. He was also probably emotionally spent from having fled from the only home he had known and from experiencing a range of emotions from the murder he had just committed.

Question 9. The narrative is very brief when describing Reuel's actions, which makes it important to make good observations. Reuel responded to his daughters' story with immediate concern for the traveler who assisted them. The first recorded question he had was about the lack of hospitality that his daughters had shown. The text says that Moses agreed to stay with Reuel, implying that there was a request that he stay with the household (Ex 2:21). The implication is that Reuel extended hospitality beyond giving Moses a meal and sending him on his way. He instead offered the protection, relationships and provision that came with joining a household. Reuel gave his daughter in marriage, which solidified the relationship between Moses and Reuel's household.

This question is designed to help the group be very specific about the cost of being hospitable. Focus the discussion on the actual financial costs of providing food and shelter for another person and the possible relational costs of taking in a foreigner.

Question 10. There are multiple names for Reuel recorded in Scripture. Most will know him as Jethro, which is the more familiar name. However, it appears that Reuel and Jethro are indeed the same person. The multiple names could reflect tribe names verses clan names (T. Desmond Alexander and David W. Baker, *Dictionary of the Old Testament: Pentateuch* [Leicester: IVP, 2003]).

Reuel was not concerned that Moses was a different ethnicity. He welcomed Moses into his household and gave his daughter in marriage— seemingly without hesitation. Hospitality was not limited to members of one's own household or tribe or clan. Reuel extended it beyond those boundaries to include a foreigner.

Exodus 2:22 is filled with important elements: Zipporah and Moses had a son, who they named Gershom. The name is a play on words from the Hebrew words for "alien" (*ger*) and "there" (*shom*). This was Moses' self-understanding. He was a foreigner, meaning that he was of a different ethnicity or from a different geographical place. The word "alien" (*ger*) is used ninety-one times in the Old Testament. Most of the usages refer to a non-Israelite who had taken up residence in the household of an Israelite. This person was dependent on that household and, in many cases, was seen as a vulnerable member of society. In this case, Moses was the alien who was dependent on the household of his father-in-law. Moses' life as a foreigner who had been taken into a household foreshadows the ways that Israel would be expected to act as written in the law.

Questions 12-13. The elements of hospitality that are seen in these two passages are urgent sacrifice and service, extended in particular to those in need. It may be that you will need to revisit question 4 in order to get at some of the attitudes that may need redeeming. It will also be good to revisit the group discussion question regarding strangers in the community. Help the group be as specific as possible in question 13 so that each person is thinking about their opportunities to extend hospitality.

Study 2. Loving Out of Remembrance. Deuteronomy 10:12-22; 24:10-22.
Purpose: To grasp that hospitality is an extension of God's character in our own lives and a response to the grace that has been given to us.
Group discussion. Help the group think deeply about this question. It will be too easy for the group to share broad and unspecific things that God has done or even very broad characteristics of God. Too often we, as believers, attribute our current status or situation in life to be a result of our exceptional talent, wisdom or extra hard work. It is true that these are a part of our lives; however, it is also true that the opportunities, experiences and blessings that have contributed to our life situation are God's handiwork. Help guide the group toward identifying all of God's acts of grace in their lives.
Personal reflection. This question should challenge each individual as well. It is designed to help people connect God's character with how they live each day. Are there specific ways in which they live that would cause others around them to stop and pause and be drawn to God? Or are the ways we live indistinguishable from the ways of the world? It may be helpful to choose one or two characteristics that arose in the group discussion, and then challenge the group to reflect specifically on those characteristics in their own lives.
Question 1. The idea of this question is to help the group see that God has done all of the work in regard to Israel. He loved them first, he set his affections on them, and he chose them. Israel was God's initiative, and their existence is not from the merits of their own character. Verses 14-15 specifically get at this dynamic between God and Israel, but God's grace can even be seen in the giving of the law (verse 13). The law was described by Moses as being for the people's own good, it was an act of grace and love by God toward Israel. God's character is seen most acutely in verses 14-15 as well. His role as Creator God is depicted here, with his power and authority over all of creation being pictured.
Question 2. This is a very important question because it lays the groundwork for understanding the rest of the passage and the entire study. It shows the connection between God's gracious, active character and the lives of his people. Verse 12 sets forth the kind of life that Israel is

required to exhibit in direct response to God's grace. The law came after God's mercy and grace through liberating Israel from Egypt. The law was the response then to God's love. He chose Israel for a purpose in the world (see Ex 19:3-6), loved them first and then expected their lives to reflect his own character to the world. Thus verse 12 requires that Israel fear the Lord, walk in his ways, love him, serve him and observe his commands. This verse gets at every aspect of Israel's response to God. It highlights the mind, the soul, the heart and the actions. The phrase "walk in his ways" was a common expression in the Old Testament, used to depict a certain lifestyle that was compatible with who God is. In verse 16, Moses reminded the Israelites of their less-than-adequate response to God at times in the desert. They were stiff-necked and stubborn at times, refusing to trust and obey. So here Moses was reminding them that they were to live in a different way, a way of faith and obedience as they entered the Promised Land.

Question 3. This is a crucial question to the whole topic of hospitality. Frequently in the Old Testament (in various genres) these three groups are referred to together: the orphans (or fatherless), the widows and the aliens are grouped with one another due to their common vulnerability. They were not necessarily poor, but they were certainly vulnerable. The most common characteristic was their weak status and the ease with which others could take advantage of them. They were cut off from the standard social connections (family kinship structures), connections that made it feasible to survive, flourish and avoid the slip into poverty. The potential to lack land—the predominant requirement for survival— was great for all three of these groups.

The key point that the group needs to grasp is that these groups of people represented the most vulnerable segments of society. They often were taken advantage of in the court system. They had limited economic means, and they were ripe for oppression and injustice.

The other crucial aspect of this question is to help the group connect God's character to the plight of these most vulnerable groups. Moses reminded the Israelites that the heart of God is stirred by the plight of these people. He acts on their behalf to extend hospitality and to make sure they have provisions and justice.

Question 4. This question is also attempting to connect for the group the gracious acts of God and the subsequent actions of his people. Moses was reminding the Israelites of their experience of economic, spiritual, physical and emotional oppression in their time of slavery in Egypt. They were in the same situation as aliens currently in their midst. The potential that Israel would forget their own experience and oppress aliens and/or take advantage of their situation for their own benefit certainly existed. Thus Moses reminded them of the grace of God that brought them out of Egypt and delivered them from oppression. It was because they knew what it was like, and because they knew that it was only through God's grace they were free, that they could respond with compassion and love toward the aliens in their midst.

The connection between remembering our own experiences of God's grace and extending compassion and hospitality to others is the heart of this study, the heart of Israel's experience and the heart of the gospel of Jesus Christ.

Question 5. This is an application question designed to help the group take the study out of the theoretical arena and into the practical arena of their own lives. Sometimes, people are reluctant to think of specific instances because it keeps the application of God's Word at arms-length. As a leader, try to gently challenge them to respond honestly and specifically.

This may be a time when a short time of personal reflection is needed before the group shares. It may also be that the group needs to stop and respond in prayer at this point as well.

Question 6. Most scholars believe that the law codes are collections of laws that are representative, not comprehensive. They list certain cases and laws that are not always connected to one another. In this passage we have a grouping of laws that relate to the needy people groups in the community, but verse 16 seems out of place in the midst of this. However, this is not uncommon in the law codes. This law is not dealt with in this study because it relates to an entirely different topic. Remind the group that it is not being ignored because it is unimportant, but merely because it is not connected topically to the laws surrounding it.

The groups of people that are included in this section of the law codes are: neighbors in financial need, those in poverty, hired men (who are also poor), aliens, the fatherless and the widow, as well as the fathers and children.

All these groups share similar life situations as those in question 3. The important items in this question are that all these groups are needy—whether for money, food or shelter—and they are vulnerable to those in positions of power and influence. The people with means in this passage have the potential to exploit those in need and use them for their own benefit. It will be helpful for the group to take each section individually and to carefully look at each circumstance.

Question 7. It is again advisable to answer this question by taking each section individually and attempting to discern what is behind the particular law.

The law in Deuteronomy 24:10-13, 17 seems to get at preserving the dignity of the borrower and also addressing the physical needs of the poor. The creditor is not allowed to enter into the borrower's home to take whatever item is being offered as a pledge. This preserves the dignity of the borrower.

The other aspect of this law is to protect the borrower. God's heart is clearly soft toward the person in need here. If a cloak is offered as collateral because of financial hardship, God is aware that this needy person will still have need of that cloak for his physical condition. God is concerned that the situation of the poor is not exploited and that the situation of the wealthy is not pressed for more advantage.

Again, Deuteronomy 29:14-15 is concerned with the plight of those who are poor and needy. A hired man could be an alien (a foreigner who is residing with the Israelites), or an Israelite who had fallen on hard times and was forced to hire himself out to survive. In either case, the hired man is not one of means but of poverty. We glimpse God's heart in this law, because God is aware of the special needs of the poor and how the system in place might very well work against them. A poor man needs his wages more frequently because he is living "paycheck to paycheck." God is very concerned that his people do not take advantage of others.

Question 8. Motivational clauses are not unique to Israel's law codes, but the content of the motivational clauses is unique. The references to Israel's own experience as a motivation for a certain way of life and the references to the character of God serve as the bulk of the motivational clauses in Israel's law codes. There are four motivational clauses in this passage (verses 13, 15, 18 and 22). The first two deal with the consequences of the actions. When a creditor acts with compassion, the borrower will see that as a righteous act and will think highly of that person. This will certainly further the mission of Israel as a witness to the nations. In verse 15, the consequences are the reverse: when the worker is not paid his wages each day, that worker may cry out to God against the employer for his lack of compassion or his exploitation. This motivational clause puts the lack of compassion into the realm of sin.

The last two motivational clauses use Israel's own experience as the motivation for obedience. Remembering their state of slavery, God's grace and mercy in delivering them is what should motivate Israel to respond in similar ways to others.

Question 9. Deuteronomy 24:19-22 are known as "gleaning laws" because they refer to the practice of the poor and needy "gleaning" what is left in a field after the harvesters and owners of the field have collected the main harvest. These three examples represent all of Israel's main crops (grain, olives, wine), thereby showing that, in all areas of life, provision for the poor should be considered. The abundance of the fields, trees and vines are to be celebrated but not hoarded. Instead, the harvesters should be generous and open-handed with the excess, making sure that it is used for those truly in need.

The other aspect of this section that God is concerned about is the greed and material acquisition of his people. These laws clearly show that excess is not to be acquired and hoarded for the benefit of one's self. The fields, trees and vines produce an abundance, but only what is needed is to be taken.

Help the group understand that God is not only concerned that his people help the poor and needy but that his people put limits to their consumption and material acquisition.

Question 10. The intent of this question is to highlight the costly nature of compassion and hospitality. When people of means exploit others, the wealthier people end up with great benefits to themselves. If the creditor in 24:10 is allowed to enter the borrower's house, he may choose something as credit that would benefit him even more if the loan defaulted. If the employer does not pay the laborer his pay every day, he can hold onto that money longer, thus putting it to use and making more money for himself. If the harvesters go back over the field a second time, they will harvest much more and have greater food or more income from selling it.

There is a cost to compassion, and there is an opportunity cost to hospitality. The people of God must be willing to give up some economic wealth or a more comfortable situation in order to avoid exploiting the poor and to protect the most vulnerable groups of society.

Question 11. This question has been addressed in various ways in previous notes. It is important to help the group grasp the concept that the way they treat the most vulnerable members of society must be in response to the grace that they have received from the Lord. We must see the hand of God in our lives and respond to others out of compassion and hospitality.

Question 12. Help the group be specific with this question. It is not helpful for hospitality to be left as a nondescript, nebulous concept without practical application. Go back over the passages and list the actual actions that are considered extending hospitality.

Question 13. This could be a difficult and touchy question. As a leader, you will have to be discerning about the group and whether or not the group is ready for this question. The intent of the question is to get at the ways that wealthier believers may benefit from our world's systems while the vulnerable people in our societies suffer from the same systems. Some examples may be the opportunity to participate in the real estate market, where someone can acquire additional wealth simply by owning something. This additional wealth can be put to work and produce even more wealth. Whereas, the poor in our society, who do not have a certain amount of capital in the first place, cannot participate in the acquisition of wealth through real estate. Participation in the stock market benefits those who have a certain amount of means already.

Helping the group through this question will involve a level of discernment and good small group communication skills. The idea is not to condemn or to have a political discussion but to bring to the surface ways that the most vulnerable in our society are overlooked, and to highlight our responsibility to extend hospitality in very concrete ways to those folks.

Question 14. This is a follow-up question to question 13. This is where, as a group, you want to address hospitality communally and not just individually. Approaching the topic of hospitality in the deep ways that this passage requires is overwhelming if only viewed individualistically. The people of God are a community, and the ways in which we extend hospitality must also be done as a corporate body.

Study 3. Kindness Beyond Expectations. Ruth 2; 4:13-22.
Purpose: To be willing to go above and beyond basic cultural expectations in serving others.

Group discussion. This is a difficult question because it requires the group to observe expectations that are unstated but present within their church community or other faith community (a small group or a campus fellowship). The goal of this question is to highlight what hospitality looks like in the community. If the group is having difficulty answering the question, prompt them to think about what is normally expected when someone new attends their small group or church, or even when someone new moves into their neighborhood. The reason for this question is to set a standard or a norm of hospitality in today's faith communities and to compare it to the hospitality seen in this chapter of Ruth.

Personal reflection. Once the standards have been articulated above, then each person can evaluate how faithful they are to these norms of hospitality.

Question 1. This question is very important so be sure to spend an adequate amount of time on it. It is designed to bring the group members into the story itself on an emotional level.

Ruth is a member of two of the most vulnerable groups within ancient Israelite society: she is a foreign widow. Although she may have been a convert to the Israelite religion (Ruth 1:16), she was still a foreigner in terms of ethnicity. This is a key part of the story, and the author continues to highlight it by referring to Ruth as the Moabitess. She had no income, was poor and had no options for work or provision. In Israelite society, the widow was extremely vulnerable, open to being exploited and in danger of poverty and starvation. Yet Ruth was willing to do whatever it took to provide for herself and for her mother-in-law. She may not have been familiar with the gleaning laws of Israel, which dictated that farmers should leave some of the harvest behind for those who were gleaning (Lev 19:9-10), thus she attempted to find someone who would regard her with favor.

The description of Boaz in these first few verses is important to the whole story of the book of Ruth. Boaz was a relative of Elimelech, Naomi's husband. Although, Levirate marriage does not occur in this story in the strict sense, it is important to the story that Boaz was a relative of Elimelech, thereby having some obligation to the widows. Boaz was described as a man of good standing, painting a picture of a man who was a good citizen and was thought of highly in the community. He also had land and servants to work the land, thus creating the picture of a man of some means.

Question 2. Ruth willingly entered a difficult situation for the sake of providing for her family. Gleaning in the fields where men were working could be dangerous for her physically. She was a young woman without a husband. She was a foreigner, who may have been in danger of exploitation, and the work of gleaning for a young woman would have been physically straining.

Question 3. The first thing to notice is the emphasis on her foreign ethnicity. Even though she may have been a convert, her ethnic identity was the first thing to be mentioned. Yet they also were aware of the hard work that she had done and her tireless dedication to the task. The men had a level of respect for Ruth. She had done a very difficult thing, leaving her home to be beside her mother-in-law and to provide for her. She had taken on the role of providing for her family.

These points are important to uncover as the study moves toward personal application. There are many people in our communities who have undertaken difficult things in order to provide for their families.

Question 4. Ask the group to carefully list all the ways that Boaz cared in concrete ways for Ruth. Boaz gave Ruth official permission to stay and glean in his fields. He encouraged her to stay in his fields so that he could provide for her, and he made it beneficial for her to stay in one place. He gave her an official place among his own servant girls, which indicates some special position for her among the household. Boaz also graciously provided Ruth with water, which would have been jealously guarded due to the difficulty of finding and drawing it.

In 2:10, Ruth asked Boaz why he was so generous to a foreigner. The implication is that others didn't act this way toward foreigners and that his actions were beyond the expectations or norms for the rest of society. Foreigners were not often treated this generously.

In Ruth 2:14-16, Boaz's provision continued with his invitation to share in the evening meal, which implies that she was included with his harvesting party. In addition, she was protected from possible molestation by the men with whom she was working so closely. Because she was a widow and did not belong to the field's owner, she was vulnerable to advances from men in the field, yet Boaz was kind enough to think through this and to make special stipulations.

In the gleaning laws of Israel, the gleaners were given the right to gather what was left of the grain only after the harvesters had gone through the field. Boaz gave Ruth permission to gather sheaves as the harvesters went along; this ensured her even more success in gleaning. Boaz had gone above and beyond the required gleaning laws in order to provide for Ruth. He went even further in verse 16 by telling his workers to pull out some stalks from the bundles and leave them for her. Boaz was intentionally going beyond the required hospitality and giving her a portion of his harvest. Boaz would inevitably lose some of his own harvest.

Question 5. Boaz's character is revealed in these verses as one marked by kindness, respect, faith, generosity and grace. If we could overhear others speaking of us, what might we hear? Are there concrete things to be seen in our lives that would spur others to speak of our generosity or grace?

Question 6. Ruth responded with great thankfulness for all that Boaz did for her. In 2:10 she bowed down with her face to the ground, which was a sign of great respect and humility. She knew that Boaz had gone beyond the required actions for gleaning and she was grateful.

Question 7. The amount of grain that Ruth gathered was an incredible amount for a gleaner. This is illustrated by Naomi's actions and is a testament to the faithfulness of Boaz and his men, and to the hard work of Ruth.

Question 8. The end of this chapter implies that the generosity of Boaz allowed Ruth and Naomi to survive and flourish. Because of his actions, Ruth and Naomi survived in the most vulnerable position in society.

Question 9. This is a fitting end to the story of Ruth and Boaz. Boaz was generous and extended hospitality beyond what was expected. Because he provided for Ruth—and ended up marrying her, giving her and Naomi a secure future—these two women thrived and became the ancestors of King David and, ultimately, of Christ Jesus. This is a great place for the group to stop and reflect on the hand of God in this story and the blessing of God that was extended through the faithfulness of his people. Because Boaz was generous beyond reason, there was a Moabite woman in the line of King David and of Jesus.

Question 10. This is a good time to review the group discussion at the beginning of the study. What were the expectations of hospitality? How can we go beyond these to extend the same kind of hospitality that Boaz did? The key to this question is to tie in the fact that Ruth was a foreigner, who would probably not have been treated well. Who are these people in our own lives?

The second important feature of this application question is recognizing that we do not know the plans of God in this world. We cannot presume to know who God is going to use for what part of his plans of redemption.

Study 4. A Heart of Hospitality. Psalm 146.

Purpose: To identify the places or people we trust in instead of God, and to ground us in the reasons why God is trustworthy.

Group discussion. The opening question is to encourage your group to honestly evaluate where your community places its trust. This is a great opportunity for the leader to help the group think deeply about the things in life that rival God for our attention, devotion and hope. For example, in Western culture, education, money and politics can all be places where people put their trust.

Personal reflection. Try to be as honest as possible. Identify what you worry about the most, what fills your budget or checkbook, what you spend time on primarily. It is likely that what you worry about the most is connected to the object of your trust and/or hope. In a similar fashion, the object of our money and time is often the very object of our trust and hope. Perhaps these objects are entertainment, education, politics or relationships. Identifying where we place our trust is an excellent starting point for reading this psalm.

Question 1. This is more of an exercise than a question. It is a way of helping group members enter into the psalm with their hearts and not just with their heads. Psalms are poetic and musical. They are written with the intent of influencing our entire selves. It is more helpful to have the leader read the psalm slowly several times with no response from the group. After the reading is finished, have the group share impressions, thoughts, feelings. Try to help the group avoid intellectual comments or responses about interpreting the psalm at this point.

Question 2. The psalmist begins his psalm with praise and an exhortation for all to praise the Lord. The psalmist is speaking a corporate command. He then transitions into the first person and states his intentions toward the Lord. He dedicates himself to the praise of the Lord throughout his entire life. The beginning of this psalm sets the stage for the rest of it. Praise is where we should begin, and praise of God is the foundation on which all else is built.

Question 3. The entire psalm is one big contrast between putting one's trust in the things of the world or in the Lord himself. The psalmist gives the readers two options: the world as represented by "princes" and "mortal men" (v. 3) and the Lord (v. 5). He expands his argument by giving characteristics of both (vv. 3-4, 6-10). The characteristics develop the argument by persuading the reader of the folly of trusting in the world and the wisdom of trusting in the Lord. Help the group study the structure of the psalm so that they see how it all fits together to develop a persuasive argument for the reader.

Question 4. The psalmist uses two words/phrases to depict the places of trust one could choose: "princes" and "mortal men." "Princes" definitely brings to mind the royal house and the ruling structure, while "mortal men" seems to refer to trusting in people in general. The psalmist is not being comprehensive but representative. The psalmist gives only two reasons in his argument against trusting the things of the world. First, nothing in this world is able to save humans from the sinful condition in which they are mired. Second, the things of this world are not eternal. They will perish, and all the plans and grand ideas of people and institutions of the world will be lost.

Question 5. The psalmist focuses first on God's creation characteristics, the fact that he is the creator of everything. His power overshadows and almost makes a mockery out of the thought of trusting in princes and mortal men. Then, the psalmist describes God in terms of his compassion and concern for the vulnerable. The psalmist chooses to contrast God with the world by illuminating God's compassion for the weak. All the groups he mentions are groups that have been referenced before in previous studies: the oppressed, the hungry, the imprisoned, the blind, the bowed down, the alien, the fatherless, the widow.

Question 6. This question is designed to step beyond academic observations of the text and to engage it again with the heart. The list of characteristics that the psalmist uses will likely evoke in us some emotional response. It may be that the group needs to stop and listen for this reaction for a few moments. This is a great time to hear the hearts of the group members. Some may respond to the imprisoned and others to the blind. Some may respond to a group because of their own current situation while others may respond out of compassion for a certain group of people.

Question 7. The psalm contrasts the transitory, unstable nature of humanity and the world's systems with the power of the Creator. God has made all things in heaven and on Earth, and he remains faithful forever. This verse highlights the power of God: Because God has the power as the Creator and he remains faithful forever, there is no reason why we should not choose to put our trust in him.

It may be helpful to remind the group of the opening discussion and to compare the things that they shared with the power of the Creator. When politicians, schools, jobs or relationships are compared to the One who has created all things and sustains all things, there is truly no contest. Help the group wrestle with the practical implications of God being the Creator. How does his power, which is exhibited in the creation, manifest itself every day in our lives?

Question 8. This question hearkens back to question 6. The elements of hospitality that have been seen in previous studies are, I hope, beginning to be solidified in the group's understanding. Being aware of the most vulnerable people and their very concrete needs, and then meeting those needs in sacrificial ways, is at the heart of hospitality. Again, this list of characteristics emphasizes the people groups most at risk of being taken advantage of or oppressed in the ancient world. It is not much different in our modern world.

Question 9. Help the group wrestle with the characteristics of God that the members have chosen as the ones that emphasize his worthiness to receive our trust. It is a bit counterintuitive to choose God's compassionate heart for the vulnerable as an argument for putting our trust and hope in him. Many of us would choose to emphasize God's power, his ability to control all things, his transcendence or his saving work. Yet the psalmist chooses compassion for the vulnerable. Make sure the group does not pass this by but wrestles with it.

The psalmist may have chosen these characteristics because so many of us will find ourselves in a situation of weakness and vulnerability at one point or another. For those who live in affluent settings, getting at this concept may be more difficult since we do not face the same kind of physical vulnerability as is depicted in this psalm. Yet, for all of us, we experience times of distress, confusion, discouragement and pain. For others, these descriptions (vv. 7-9) are all too familiar. They struggle with physical, economic and judicial vulnerability. The fact that God is compassionate toward these groups of people (and us in those situations) and acts on their behalf gives hope. It is easier to place trust in this kind of a God, knowing that he does not forget those in trouble but acts for their benefit.

Question 10. The appearance of the words *righteous* and *wicked* may seem strange to modern readers who connect these terms to actions rather than faith. The psalm is contrasting those who put their trust, hope and faith in God with those who trust the world and its institutions of power and influence. The object of their trust becomes the determining factor between being righteous or wicked. The righteous are those who trust in God; they are not just people who happen to choose a "good" act. Likewise, the wicked are those who have turned away from God and are attempting to find their hope in the world.

God loves those who are in relationship with him and are placing their hope and trust in him. Yet he frustrates the paths of those who look to the world or to other human beings for their hope. Their way will always be frustrated because those things are not worthy of their trust.

Question 11. This is the beginning of a time of application. The purpose of the question is to bring the group back into the text emotionally. There has been discussion about everyone being in situations of vulnerability and the hope that comes from a God who cares about that. This question is designed to help the group be honest with one another and to build community with one another through opening up their lives a bit. Help the group try and identify where they see themselves. Some may see themselves as the oppressed while others may see themselves as the psalmist who is filled with praise.

Make sure the group does not skip part two of this question. The main point of the psalm is that God cares for those in vulnerable positions—and that includes the situations that group members have shared. God acts on their behalf! Help the group to interact with the hopeful words of the psalm.

The group may need to respond by ending the study right here and praying for one another. It may be necessary to respond to the heartfelt sharing of members by allowing more discussion. As a leader, be alert to the movement of the Holy Spirit as you respond to the group.

Question 12. This final question moves the group from focusing on their own situations of vulnerability and God's compassion for them to the situations of others. This question may not feel right depending on the discussion and sharing from the previous question. If the group has emotionally connected with question 11, then stay there and finish the study in that vein. However, if the group did not connect at a deeper level with question 11 or if the group members did not feel as if they were in vulnerable places right then, then proceed with this question. Help the group to focus outward on the love and compassion God has for the weak and vulnerable.

Study 5. Fasting the Lord's Way. Isaiah 58.

Purpose: To understand that following God includes caring about injustice and oppression and that our Christian lives must reflect this concern.

Group discussion. Help the group think through all the disciplines or activities that occur in either their church, small group or campus fellowship that they perceive to be ways of seeking God. Some examples may be prayer, Bible study, worship, fasting, etc. The idea of the question is to have group members think deeply about what it means to seek God.

Personal reflection. If you are leading a group through this study, you may want to use this question as a time of silent reflection with a brief time for sharing afterward. The question is designed to take the group discussion question from the realm of theory into the personal arena.

Question 2. In these initial verses, the assumed purpose of a fast is disclosed. However, it is not explicit but rather implicit in the verses. You may have to help the group wrestle with verses 1-3 in order to find out what the people of Israel thought of a fast. These verses are set in the context of temple worship, because Israel's worship revolved around the activities of the temple. The temple was where they sought out the Lord; it was the place where they came to sacrifice and put right their relationship with the Lord; it was the place of prayer and fellowship. Help the group try to stay in the text and in the temple worship setting of Israel without jumping to our current church context.

The people of Israel seem to be seeking God and eager for connection to him. They ask him for decisions in prayer and desire relationship with him. Verse 3 implies that the purpose of their fasting is to get God's attention, to connect with him and put forth their petitions.

It may be helpful to briefly mention that these are worthy pursuits and not much different than our own intentions today.

Question 3. This question gets at the crux of God's complaint against the people. Isaiah was a prophet in the eighth century B.C. to the southern kingdom of Judah. This was a difficult time, which ended in the fall of the Northern Kingdom of Israel and massive destruction within Judah. The prophets of this time focused on the rebellion of God's people and Israel's coming punishment through the world powers amassing around them. Many of the complaints of the prophets circulated around the inconsistency of Israel's religious behavior, the practices of the cult and the social situation within the nation. This passage wrestles with these aspects of life in Israel.

In verses 3-5, Israel tries to get the Lord's attention through their fasting or cultic responsibilities, but God does not seem to answer or to draw near. God's questioning of the people is directed at their perception of fasting as only a ritual without other consequences. In Israel's perspective, they only needed to go through the motions of fasting and fulfill their religious requirements at the temple in order for God to hear them.

Question 4. The passage is structured to alternate between the types of activities that are consistent with the Lord's understanding of worship and the consequences of engaging in these life choices. It is a poetic structure which moves through the main elements of acceptable worship.

Verse 6 focuses on societal dynamics, implying that acceptable fasting and worship has much to do with how God's people interact with society. In seeking God, his people must not ignore those who find themselves as victims of unjust structures but instead be instruments of justice in those very systems.

Verse 7 moves from societal structures and systems to the physical needs of humanity. Acceptable worship—the Lord's kind of fasting—includes addressing in concrete ways the physical needs of others: hunger, homelessness and nakedness.

Verses 9-10 reiterate the very elements already mentioned in previous verses. These two verses tie together the societal systems with the most basic of human needs: oppression and hunger. Yet, these verses add the cessation of malicious talk and finger-pointing to the definition of acceptable worship.

Verse 13 adds the commandment of keeping the sabbath to the definition of an acceptable fast. It will be important to help the group think through the purpose of the sabbath in order to understand why it is so important to seeking God. Yet, in this passage, it is implied that the people were not keeping the sabbath but were choosing to go about their lives as they determined on God's day. They were choosing to do as they pleased rather than following the sabbath law, including speaking idle words.

Question 5. Isaiah 58 is in the section of the book that focuses on the restoration of Israel and their coming hope. In the first half of Isaiah, the prophet's words describe the coming of the Lord's wrath in response to Israel's rebellion. The words of judgment were not only for Israel but also for those nations who had not recognized Yahweh and had acted unjustly and oppressed others. The focus of Isaiah 58 is now on the restoration of Israel *after* the coming judgment and exile. The verses in this passage that describe the consequences of acceptable worship connect with this thread of restoration. If Israel would act in ways that are consistent with the Lord's character and his definition of what it means to seek him, then they would experience the kind of restoration and redemption that is pictured throughout this section of the book. The nation as a whole would experience renewal after their judgment.

It is important to see the corporate nature of this passage. The community as a whole must seek the Lord in these ways—not just individuals.

This will be a crucial key in the group's understanding of the whole concept of hospitality. It is corporate as well as individual.

The poetic structure of this passage includes God's response to those who would seek him in these ways, to those whose worship would include justice, would address the needs of others and would keep the sabbath. Verses 8-9 highlight the restored relationship with God: God would answer their calls, their prayers, and he would come to their aid in distress. The description of God saying "Here am I" is a wonderful picture of the restored relationship. In exile, the people would question whether or not God was with them anymore, yet in the restoration, he would remind them of his presence with them. This was the land that was promised to their ancestors. They had been exiled from it, but because of their future acceptable worship, they would be returned to their land.

Question 6. It is crucial to connect the kind of life that God's people live with their spiritual lives and their relationship with God. Many times, Christians believe that it is only through Bible study and prayer that one can come closer to God. However, this passage connects our interaction with the world and with others to our spiritual growth. It is when we engage in helping others and bringing justice and redemption to the world that we are engaged in the work of God.

This may be a good time to ask someone for an example. There may be people in the group who have great stories about how ministering in these ways affected their ability to seek the Lord.

Question 7. This is a personal reflection question to get at the reasons why we have difficulty seeking God in these ways. This question may bring about significant conversation related to engaging societal structures or meeting physical needs. Try to stay with what the text has to say, steering the group back to the text. *What is God saying here in this passage?*

Question 8. This passage has described what it means to seek the Lord, yet the answers to the group discussion question at the beginning of the study may have only included individual actions and "spiritual" activities. This is a point where the group needs to wrestle with the concrete understanding of what this looks like in a modern church context. What does it mean to loose the chains of injustice in your community? What does it mean to address societal structures as well as basic human needs? What does it mean to keep the sabbath and not do as you please? The leader must help the group to move out of theory and abstract answers into the more concrete discussions that the question begs.

Do not forget to wrestle both with the corporate and individual implications of the passage and of the question.

Question 9. God uses these images: light (v. 10), a garden (v. 11), construction (v. 12) and riding on the heights (v. 14). Help the group to identify the images first and then begin to interpret what the images would have brought to mind for ancient Israel. Light and darkness are frequent images to describe the Lord's and Israel's experience. Their time in exile and the destruction of their land would have been seen as darkness, but the restoration would be seen as coming out of that darkness into the light of a restored life in the land and a restored relationship with God.

The garden is also a frequent metaphor for the prophets and the psalmists. It depicts fruitfulness and abundance in a land that, at times, was difficult. The provision of never-ending water would have brought to mind the Lord's goodness and the land that they had been promised. It would have pictured a nation that was doing well.

Because the city of Jerusalem and the surrounding areas were decimated before the exile, the images of construction, repair and rebuilding would have been a picture of hope. Jerusalem was the holy city, the city of David and the dwelling place of God in the temple. When it was destroyed, the security and honor of the people was lost as well as their trust in the presence of the Lord with them. Yet God gave them a picture of rebirth; the city would be reestablished and restored.

The last image is of riding on the heights, which would have been an image of security. These images were used to instill hope about the time of restoration but they were tied to the obedience of Israel in keeping the right kind of spirituality. Israel must seek God by these ways if they were to experience this kind of renewal.

Question 10. This question is designed to connect this passage about seeking God to the concept of hospitality. The incredible point of this text is that when we extend hospitality to others, there is a direct connection to the vitality of our own spiritual lives. If our lives are characterized by the elements of hospitality, then our worship is acceptable to God and our relationship with him is vibrant.

Question 11. This is designed to be a very concrete question. It may be that group members need to further process the connection between hospitality, worship and the vibrancy of our spirituality, but it may also be that the group is ready to think specifically about extending hospitality in these ways. Be discerning as the leader.

Study 6. Dwelling in Service. Matthew 25:31-46.

Purpose: To wrestle with the relationship between serving the needy and how that manifests faith, and to challenge each person to serve in concrete ways.

Group discussion. Many times people will associate "righteous" people with the absence of certain acts in their lives, such as avoiding the use of alcohol or drugs or pre- or extra-marital sexual activity. It may not be likely that the group will identify actions directed at the poor or vulnerable members of society. The idea of this question is to bring to the surface our limited view or understanding of being "righteous" or "cursed." This is a very open-ended question with no "right" or "wrong" answers, so let the group discuss and list without too much direction.

Personal reflection. This question also focuses on one's understanding of the term *righteous.* This question should enable each person to reflect on his/her own life and try to identify what he/she perceives to be "righteous" elements. This should highlight one's definition of "righteous," which will be helpful as the study progresses.

Question 1. It may be important to mention that all of Matthew 24—25 took place as Jesus and his disciples were in Jerusalem after his triumphal entrance into the city. They had just been at the temple, and they were discussing the significant events to come. Jesus spent time discussing the signs that the historical climax was near but then transitioned into various parables about being ready for this period. It was within this context that Jesus continued the teaching with the description of the sheep and goats.

It is significant to notice that the type of teaching shifts a bit from a parable to direct teaching. Jesus did not begin this description with the characteristic phrase, "The kingdom of God will be like . . ." as he had in the previous two parables. Instead, this part of chapter 25 has a different feel. Jesus had finished the parables and seemed to be describing the end directly. He did, however, still use the metaphor of sheep and goats.

The characters in Matthew 25:31-33 include the Son of Man, who will be returning in all his glory. He will be accompanied by his angels, and the context is understood (from the larger literary context) to be a judgment. Jesus is pictured here as the King, whereas in most Jewish parables the king is God. The nations are also pictured in this scene. All the nations will be gathered before the throne of Jesus. It is not merely the Jews who will face this event but all the nations.

Question 3. This passage is structured as a contrast, which is the main literary device in the passage. By finding and highlighting all the contrasting words and phrases, group members will be able to see this literary device.

Some direct contrasts include: left and right, sheep and goats, blessed and cursed, inheritance and eternal fire, kingdom and eternal fire, the image of heaven versus the devil, eternal punishment and eternal life, righteous and cursed. These words are scattered throughout the passage, and the impact is that a sharp division is being made.

There are further contrasts that are not within direct contrasting words. The whole idea of the hungry, the thirsty, the sick, the imprisoned, the naked and the stranger either being cared for or being ignored is itself a contrast. The action is either toward helping the needy or not. Again, a sharp division is being drawn in this passage. Something has either happened or not, and because an action has either happened or not, a person will be defined as a sheep or a goat.

Help the group work all the way through the passage so that the literary device of contrasts is seen.

Question 4. The group may not have any clear answers here, but it is helpful to try and wrestle with the distinction between these animals and the perceived significance of using these animals. The background and historical and cultural context of the time is helpful here.

Sheep and goats often grazed together, but some scholars believe that they were separated at night, because they had different needs during the nighttime hours. Goats need warmth so they huddle together, while sheep prefer to be in the open air (Craig S. Keener, *The IVP Bible Background Commentary: New Testament* [Downers Grove, Ill.: InterVarsity Press, 1993], p. 118). Another dimension of the metaphor is the connotations associated with sheep and goats. Sheep were considered to be more valuable and may have been associated with "good" more than goats (Keener, *IVP Bible Background Commentary,* p. 18). Again, because of these cultural connotations, Jesus' audience would have easily connected the sheep and the goats with the distinction of "righteous" or "cursed."

This question is the crux of the passage. The criterion by which the sheep and goats are separated and thereby judged is the point of the passage and the place where the group needs to engage the text. The criterion is solely the manner in which the people have responded to the needs of others around them. Did the hungry person receive food or the imprisoned receive visitation?

It is important to highlight that Jesus did not point to any other criterion. The people were separated into "righteous" and "cursed" camps based on how they responded to the needs of the vulnerable and needy people around them.

Question 5. This question may seem obvious or even redundant, but it is important to highlight what the needs of these people are. The hungry did not need blankets or encouragement; they needed food. The thirsty did not need a pat on the back but a glass of water. The needs are foundational, and they were physical needs being met by the righteous in basic ways. Even for the imprisoned, the need is very foundational. When one is imprisoned, the need is not food or drink but social interaction. Having someone come to visit would touch the most basic deficiency of the prisoner.

The actions exhibited by the sheep were all standard requirements in the Jewish understanding of ethics, except for visiting the imprisoned (Keener, *IVP Bible Background Commentary,* p. 118). So, these actions and requirements would have been known and understood by the disciples (and Matthew's Jewish audience for his Gospel). Jesus was connecting the act of meeting basic and foundational needs of the most vulnerable people with the designation of righteous or cursed.

Question 6. This is the place where we as believers sometimes struggle to grasp this passage—both intellectually and in daily practice. Jesus was connecting the experience of the needy and vulnerable people with himself. There is something about meeting the needs of his people at the most basic and fundamental level that is, in essence, ministering to him as well. Jesus seemed to be trying to communicate that he is so closely attached to his people that when his creations are either cared for or ignored, he is affected as well.

This may be somewhat obvious to answer because the text is clear; however, the difficulty in this question is wrestling with the implications of this truth. The significance of seeing Jesus in the people we minister to and in the desperate situations of the needy is crucial to grasp.

Question 7. This is an application question to help the group stop and reflect on life in the middle of this study. Meeting basic needs sometimes gets shoved to the back—behind the more "spiritual" ministry of Bible study or preaching. Help the group really evaluate why it is difficult to meet basic needs, especially in our society.

Some answers may be the "hiddenness" of needs in our society, that the hungry or the homeless are unseen to most of us. This would be a wonderful place to begin discussion. It may be that we are afraid of interacting with the neediest of people, so we do not want to meet basic needs. Meeting these kinds of needs does not feel as spiritual, and many times they are long-term ministries. Often we don't want to get involved at this level because it is uncomfortable, and many other issues are raised as we begin to listen to the experiences of the needy. It can be dirty, smelly and scary to feed the hungry or visit the imprisoned.

It is imperative to try and help the group be honest and to create an environment in the group that fosters and encourages honesty. We must be honest with our fears and aversions if we are to give them to the Lord.

Question 8. The implication in these verses is that the "goats" did not make the connection between Jesus and the needy. They did not see that meeting the basic needs of people translated directly into serving Jesus. The "cursed" camp ignored the needs of the people around them.

In our own context, it may be that the "goats" ignored the vulnerable people in society as they rushed off to Bible study or worship, not understanding that to feed the hungry and clothe the naked is meeting Jesus as well.

Question 9. This is a very important question because of our tendency to try and figure out a different way to interpret this passage. It is uncomfortable to think that Jesus would separate people from one another based on the criterion of meeting the needs of the most vulnerable. One way is to spiritualize the passage. Jesus wasn't actually talking about meeting the physical needs of the hungry; he was talking about the "spiritually hungry" and the "spiritually imprisoned." Other ways that people might look at this passage include redefining the "righteous" and the "cursed" into Christians and nonbelievers. The goats are the nonbelievers, thus they do not meet the needs of others.

There are multiple ways to try and make this passage more comfortable, and some of these interpretations may have some validity. However, it is important to help the group understand our tendency to reinterpret Scripture to ease our discomfort or to justify our lifestyles. Help the group stay in that place of discomfort. It may mean that the group agrees that they don't quite understand how this passage is reconciled with salvation by faith through grace or their understanding of judgment, but that is an acceptable place to be. The crucial point is that there is something about meeting the needs of the most vulnerable that is extremely important to Jesus, and there is some connection between meeting those needs and meeting Jesus.

Question 10. Hospitality takes on a level of importance here that is serious. Often we are not willing to give it this level of importance. Rather, we relegate hospitality to a subspiritual gift and associate it with cookies and juice after worship. But hospitality takes on an eternal significance that is unsettling and disturbing to us.

It is only when we understand that there is a calling to minister to the needy, providing hospitality to the weak, the imprisoned and the hungry, that it will become important to us as well. When we understand that we will meet Jesus in the faces of the needy as we sit with them, we will live in a way that is righteous.

Question 11. The concept of corporate ministry is essential to our understanding of the Christian life, but we frequently think only in terms of the individual. When Jesus was describing this scene of judgment to the disciples, he was talking to them as a group. Together they were responsible for living like sheep. Help the group think specifically about what the group (the small group or the church community) can do to meet the basic needs of people.

Question 12. As a leader, help the group make specific plans and then help the group be accountable for those plans.

Study 7. Offering Your Resources. Mark 6:30-44.
Purpose: To identify the resources and talents that we have been given that Jesus can use to meet others' needs, if we are willing.

Group discussion. The focus in this discussion question is on the ever-increasing, all-consuming needs of the world around us. Have the group think of and list together all the needs of the community around them, adding in the larger community and the world. This will produce a daunting list of needs, which should produce a reaction of being overwhelmed. As a leader, you will want to help the group identify these kinds of feelings. The needs of the world and even the needs of just our own communities are too great for us to meet.

Personal reflection. This can be a great follow-up question. Once group members have felt the overwhelming nature of the needs around them, it is important to stop and reflect on the resources we have in order to meet those needs. This question can produce several responses. One response is to be more hopeful as individuals realize that they truly do have resources to apply to the task. The other is to see the contrast between the breadth of the need and the meager resources each person has. Both of these responses are helpful in the focus of this study.

It will be beneficial to think about all the categories of resources that one has—such as education, money, personality traits, time and spiritual gifts. These are all resources that God has given to each individual, which can be used in the work of the kingdom.

Question 1. The setting of this story is crucial to understanding the feelings and responses of the disciples. Just before this event, the disciples were sent out in pairs to minister (Mark 6:5-13). Jesus sent them out with specific instructions that would enhance their reliance on God and on the hospitality of others. During their "ministry assignments" the disciples experienced miraculous things. They preached repentance, drove out demons, anointed the sick and healed. They had apparently just returned from these ministry assignments and had gathered together again with one another and with Jesus.

Question 2. This question directly follows the discussion in the first question. Once the group has established what the disciples have experienced, it is crucial to help group members put themselves in the story and try to anticipate the feelings of the disciples. They had just returned from an amazing adventure and now they were all back together. It is likely that they had a need to be with one another and with Jesus alone in order to "debrief" their experiences, ask Jesus questions and hear one another's stories. This is similar to what short-term missionaries experience when, after they have been out on assignments in pairs, they come back to the whole group. The disciples, as with the short-term missionaries, would have a deep need to process and share their experiences.

Jesus understood this need and suggested that they go away with him to a quiet place. He knew that they needed space and time to reflect and process all that they had experienced. They needed to be with their leader in order to grasp all that had happened to them.

Yet the crowds were everywhere. People were coming and going the whole time that they were reporting to Jesus. Try to have the group imagine the scene. The disciples were gathered around Jesus and one another, all talking at once, trying to tell their stories and hear Jesus' response. But, perhaps, crowds of people kept interrupting and pushing in on them. The disciples couldn't quite get their stories out or corral Jesus' attention. Imagine the increasing disappointment and frustration that they might have been feeling.

The text does not tell us the emotions of the disciples. It may be that they were not bothered by the crowds but welcomed them. On the other hand, it makes sense that, after their experiences, they would have wanted and needed to be with Jesus. It makes sense that some of the emotions they may have been feeling would have been those of frustration, anger and disappointment. Getting group members to this place will help them in the rest of the study.

Question 3. A possible conflict that emerges, as this narrative develops, is between the needs of the crowds and the needs of the disciples. The possible conflict also would've been between the desires of the disciples and the desires of Jesus. The disciples wanted space, quiet and the full attention of Jesus. They may have had compassion on the crowds, but it also seems likely that they would have felt some internal conflict over the needs of the crowds and their needs. In either case, the compassion of Jesus shines through in the passage.

Jesus saw beyond the distraction that the crowds brought and saw their spiritual need. He knew that they were sheep without a shepherd, hungry for leadership and direction. However, Jesus was not ignorant of the needs of the disciples either. This set up a conflict of emotions and responses.

Question 4. This is a good time to stop and reflect a bit on the compassion of Jesus, because it is central to this narrative. Jesus knew the needs of the disciples. He was aware that they needed to process and debrief their ministry experiences. He was the one who suggested quiet and rest. However, his compassion was stirred when he saw the needs of the crowds. Help the group reflect on the ability of Jesus to see beyond the surface of the situation.

It will also be helpful to talk about what it means to be "sheep without a shepherd." This is the image that stirred Jesus' compassion to the point where he set aside the plan of quiet reflection that he had for the disciples. Sheep are not very bright animals. They are not self-sufficient or able to care for themselves. Sheep need a shepherd to lead them to the healthiest pastures and to clean water, otherwise they will choose to feed and drink from polluted sources. Sheep are unable to protect themselves from danger, thus the need for a shepherd. All these things probably came to mind when Jesus looked on the crowds.

Question 5. This part of the narrative reveals that the disciples had not gained Jesus' perspective but had been spending the day in the same place of frustration and anger that they had been in before. Jesus had been teaching the crowds until late in the day, and there had been no quiet reflection, rest or debriefing with Jesus for the disciples. His attention had been elsewhere. Finally, the disciples' frustration rose to the boiling point and they approached Jesus. It is easy to imagine that they came to Jesus out of this frustration, asking him to send the crowds away—finally. Because the text does not show us the motivation of the disciples, it is also possible that they saw the needs of the crowds and wanted to do something for them. The crowds were probably hungry and they needed time to go and find sustenance, so they should've been getting on their way.

The expectation of the disciples seemed to be that Jesus would agree and send the crowds on their way, so then the disciples could finally get their much-needed time with Jesus. It is doubtful that any other course of action even entered the minds of the disciples. The idea that they could do something to meet the needs of this large crowd probably did not occur to them.

The emotional content of this narrative is extremely important to the passage. Make sure to try and help the group members wrestle with the emotions of both Jesus and the disciples. Putting themselves in the story is a great way to identify with some of the characters in the narrative.

Question 6. This question is to help group members identify with the disciples. It is to highlight the tendency we have to want Jesus all to ourselves—or even to not have the inconvenience of some people or certain issues. For each of us, there are people groups (or issues) we may have a lack of compassion for. We would rather not deal with them; they are an interruption to our lives. There are people for whom the idea that we might be able to meet their needs simply does not occur to us. The focus of this question is to be honest with this and bring it to light in order to give that reaction to the Lord.

The responses might be varied, from things such as specific ethnic groups to people with certain lifestyles (wealthy people, welfare recipients, homosexuals, etc.). It might also include people with certain personality traits (introverts or loud and boisterous people, etc.). Ask the group to be thoughtful in their responses, and remind everyone that we all respond like the disciples to some degree. It is just part of our sinful condition.

Question 7. This is another question to help transition the narrative into our modern context and our personal lives. The list that was generated by the group discussion should provide the data for this question. Encourage the group to pick just one need from the list of community needs or world needs. Help group members to think about all the obstacles and stumbling blocks that one would face in trying to meet these particular needs. The idea of the question is to connect the response of the disciples to our own responses. We often respond to the needs around us with a list of obstacles and problems.

Question 8. This question is an observation question designed to get the group back into the details of the text. It is significant that he asked the disciples to identify the resources that they had as a first step. Make sure the group sees this element of the passage. It is also important to highlight that Jesus gave thanks and acknowledged the Father as a part of the miracle. This sheds light on the relationship between Jesus and the Father and the dependence on the Father that Jesus had.

The sequence of events is also very significant. Jesus took the resources that the disciples had gathered, he thanked the Father, and then he gave the fish and the loaves back to the disciples to distribute. It began with the resources among the disciples and the crowds themselves. Then, the Lord's power was applied to those resources to multiply and empower them. Last, the disciples were the ones that met the needs of the crowds through the power of the Lord.

These steps are significant because, not only was Jesus performing a miracle, he was helping the disciples debrief their ministry experiences. He had not forgotten the situation of the disciples. They needed to process their experiences. They had seen miraculous things, but when faced with the obstacle of meeting the needs of the people, they seemed to have forgotten all about the miracles they had performed in Jesus' name. They seemed to have forgotten the authority that they had been given. Jesus connected this very situation with their ministry experiences by walking them through another miracle.

Question 9. Take a few moments and think about the community's resources. This may be the small group's resources, the church community's or a broader community's, but identifying your collective resources is a good place to start. Help the group think specifically about the needs and resources in their situations and what it would look like to let Jesus empower their resources. Help the group to be creative in thinking about answers to this question.

Question 10. This is a more personal response to the study. It may be that someone is afraid that if he/she offers resources to Jesus for his kingdom work that he/she will no longer have the resources needed for him- or herself, so there may be a lack of faith in God's provision. It may be that someone lacks confidence that his/her resources can really be used. Or perhaps it is an unwillingness to part with a resource. Again, help the group to wrestle with the internal obstacles that God might be highlighting through this study.

Study 8. Feasting Through Sacrifice. Luke 22:7-30.
Purpose: To present an image of sacrificial hospitality that requires setting aside authority in order to serve others.
Group discussion. Help the group members to specifically think about people in their own contexts who are wonderful hosts. Then guide them through a discussion about the characteristics of these people that contributes to their ability to host well. The group might identify characteristics such as flexibility, compassion, thoughtfulness, a sense of the aesthetic and generosity.
Personal reflection. This question ties together both the main themes of this study. Hospitality and the idea of authority are woven together by Jesus in this passage. Help the group list the people in society today who they believe have authority. Guide the group in thinking about various segments of society: the political realm, the entertainment world, academia, media, the medical profession or the justice system. Also think about specific people in our personal lives who have authority—like parents, teachers, supervisors or mentors.

The second part of this question goes a bit deeper and tries to pinpoint the ways that authority is established and used in society. In personal reflection try to recognize how the people on the list gain and use their authority. For example, a teacher might use her authority by threatening punishment or through relationship and compassion. Does a person gain authority through competence or character, or is a person given it because of prestige or resources?

Question 1. Observing all the references to eating and drinking in the passage is an excellent way to begin to engage the passage. It will help the group see the passage as a whole and begin to discover the themes that weave throughout the passage. Encourage the group to look through the entire section and list all the times that eating and drinking are either explicitly or implicitly mentioned.

The section begins by referencing the Feast of Unleavened Bread and the preparations for eating (vv. 7-8). *Eat* is mentioned five times and *drink* two times. *Bread, wine, table* and *cup* all feature prominently in the passage as well.

A wonderful way of helping the group to engage with this question is to have them try and picture the scene and then notice all the things or feelings associated with eating and drinking. The setting, the language and the teachings of Jesus all deal with feasting and take place in the context of hospitality.

Question 3. We don't often think of Jesus as the guest, but there are times in the New Testament where Jesus is being hosted. Mary and Martha host him, he is the guest in Revelation when he stands at the door and knocks. He is a guest in this passage as well when he and his disciples are hosted by an unidentified man. Jesus did not have a place to go and celebrate the Passover. It was the Passover and the exodus to which he referred in his teachings at the Last Supper.

The man who hosted Jesus and the disciples was not named, but he was recorded in Scripture as a guest at one of the most important events of Jesus' ministry. He was probably a somewhat wealthy man due to the fact that he had an upstairs and a large guest room. The room was furnished and made ready for Jesus and the disciples. It was a large and comfortable room with enough space for the whole group to eat and recline at the table.

Question 4. Jesus referred to the covenant with Moses when he claimed the new covenant in his blood. The Jews were waiting for a new exodus when God would once again rescue his people from their oppressors. However, Jesus reminded them that they were looking for the wrong kind of deliverance. Jesus was making connections between his life and ministry and the past events of Israel. He would become the sacrificial lamb, and through his body and blood, Israel and the Gentiles would be ushered into a new relationship with God.

Question 5. This question is designed to highlight how Jesus takes common items and gives them new meaning. Wine and bread were common household items of hospitality. Bread was the staple of life and was a centerpiece in the offering of hospitality. When a guest entered the home, food and drink were immediately offered. In various cultures today, a guest has not been shown hospitality until they are given food and drink. The common symbols of hospitality—the things that travelers or guests would need the most, sustenance—are given deep significance in the Last Supper. Not only are the bread and wine connected to the Passover experience in Egypt, they are infused with spiritual meaning in the Last Supper. Food and drink, symbols of hospitality, become the reminders for all of us of the sacrificial hospitality that Jesus provided in his death and resurrection.

Question 6. This question flows directly from the preceding question and continues the theme of Jesus being the host. In this question, he becomes the ultimate host in his death and resurrection. Jesus gave the disciples a picture of what was about to happen, that he would suffer and his blood would be poured out on their behalf. He said that he was eager to celebrate the Passover meal with them before he suffered, because it would be the last time that they would eat this meal together before the full kingdom of God comes. Thus he alluded to the suffering and death that would await him, and he connected this to hospitality.

The bread and the wine, the food and the drink, are symbols of hospitality and symbols of his willing sacrifice of his own life. It was his body "given for you" and his blood "poured out for you." This is the ultimate gift of a host, to pour out his life on behalf of the guest. Providing life for others is the ultimate act of hospitality, and Jesus became the ultimate host by willingly laying down his life.

Question 7. This is the point where the group needs to stop and reflect on the amazing gift of Jesus' sacrifice. He was the ultimate host in his death and resurrection, but he continues to be the host to us individually and corporately every day. Help the group members think through the significant times in their lives when Jesus "hosted" them. These may be times of protection, revelation, healing, comfort or encouragement. This time should be one of celebration and thanks.

Question 8. The argument about the status of one another in the presence of Jesus seems unbelievably out of place. Moments before Jesus had alluded to his suffering and betrayal and now the disciples launched into a discussion about who would be the greatest. It was offensive because of the setting and their proximity to Jesus' suffering and death. In addition to this, moments earlier they had been discussing which one of them was going to betray Jesus. The fact that they were aware that one of their number was going to betray their friend and master and yet they began a disagreement over prestige seems like a direct contrast.

This question is designed to help the group continue to place themselves into the narrative. Use the question to help group members picture the whole scene and the flow of events. This is a transition part of the Last Supper.

Questions 9-10. The model of Gentile rule would have immediately come to mind for the disciples. Kings in the ancient Near East often portrayed themselves as gods, setting up harsh and authoritarian kingdoms. The rule of the Gentiles was often tyrannical and harsh, and the rulers used their authority to dominate and oppress.

Jesus contrasted the rule of the Gentile oppressor to the rule within the kingdom of God. He immediately called the disciples to reject the use of authority that they had seen in Gentile rulers for something far greater. Jesus flipped the current system of authority on its head. In ancient custom, rank and prestige was often decided by age. The oldest received the highest rank while the youngest was left with nothing. Likewise, the servant had no status or rank compared to the master. The one sitting at the table was, of course, the greatest when compared with those in the position of serving that person. Yet Jesus called the disciples to be like the youngest in the family or like the servant. He used himself as the example. Just as he served, they were to be servants as well. His followers are to use their authority in ways that are entirely different than those with authority in the world.

Question 11. This question ties the main themes of the passage together and connects with the opening questions from the beginning of the study. Help the group tie these concepts together. Jesus had all authority in heaven and on earth. Yet he willingly laid down his life as the ultimate host on behalf of all humankind.

Jesus was trying to show the disciples that the use of authority in the kingdom of God is marked by service, sacrifice and hospitality. The authority that they would have in the kingdom would be exercised far differently than how the Gentiles exercised it. Jesus knew that soon he would be gone and the disciples would be responsible for being the light of the world. Thus he wanted them to understand that they must use the power and authority that they would be given to serve others.

This concept is crucial to our understanding of the life of faith. We have been given authority by Jesus, but how are we to use this authority and the power that accompanies it? We are to exercise this power and authority in imitation of Christ—through sacrificial hospitality. We are to extend hospitality to others, all others, and this includes the vulnerable and weak and those who we are not comfortable with. Jesus' sacrifice cost him suffering and death. Our hospitality will cost us as well.

Questions 12-13. Other studies in this series have asked these questions, but here it is important for the group to emphasize sacrifice. We might be able to extend hospitality as long as it doesn't cost us anything. Help the group to be very specific in answering these questions.

Study 9. Destroying Barriers. Acts 10.
Purpose: To identify the barriers that still exist between people today, and to challenge believers to take specific steps to break down a barrier.

Group discussion. The group leader needs to prepare for the study by bringing multiple copies of the daily newspaper. Give the group a few minutes to flip through it and glance at several articles. Look for articles on immigration issues, divisions along political lines, the "achievement gap" in education, and wars and conflicts on the world scene.

Question 1. Cornelius was a Roman soldier, a centurion, stationed in Caesarea, which was the seat of the Roman governor of Judea. A centurion commanded approximately 100 men. Cornelius was, therefore, a man of some authority. In verse 7, after he received his vision, he called two servants and a soldier and sent them on an extended errand. He had the authority to command servants and soldiers. Cornelius was a God-fearer, who was devoted to Yahweh, but was not considered a complete convert because he had not gone through the act of circumcision (Keener, *IVP Bible Background Commentary,* p. 350). Cornelius had been living a righteous life, giving alms to the poor and praying to Yahweh. Not only was his righteous life known to others, including Jews (v. 22), but his attention to the poor was commended by God himself (v. 4). Cornelius had a trusting spirit even in the midst of his fear. He received a vision about asking a Jew into his home, and he immediately obeyed.

Cornelius was a family man and included his family in whatever God was doing. This would have been very natural for the culture, to include the entire family and one's circle of friends in something special. He was expectant, knowing that because God had communicated with him, God was doing something significant in his life through this man Peter. Cornelius received Peter with grace and hospitality.

There is a lot of material to cover to answer this question, so help the group to look through the narrative in sections. The idea is to paint a picture of the character of Cornelius.

Question 2. The call from God would have been difficult for both men in some respects. This would have been new territory for Cornelius. He was to find and invite a certain Jewish man into his house to bring something from God. It is likely that Cornelius had never had a Jewish person inside his home, even though he was respected by the Jews around him. He would have been aware of the solid barriers between his people and the Jewish people. Jews were strictly forbidden in the law to associate with Gentiles, thus the separation between Jews and Gentiles was a very old and established cultural and religious barrier.

The step of going to Cornelius' home was an even greater one for Peter. The idea of willingly doing what he had known all his life to be unacceptable to God would have felt incredibly risky. It was a barrier that would have been difficult to overcome and scary for Peter to address.

The point of this question is to help the group members identify with the feelings of Peter and Cornelius. This could have been a very scary and anxious time for both of them. On the other hand, both knew that God was intimately involved, and this might have brought a sense of anticipation and excitement as well.

Question 3. Barriers keep us from learning wonderful things about one another, and they imprison us in a variety of ways. When a barrier is removed there is freedom to learn and grow with one another. We become better people because we are interacting with people that may see the world from a new or different perspective. It is hard for us to imagine what it would be like without barriers or walls between people, so it may be easier to focus on just one relationship.

Question 4. This is another observation question that forces the group to look at large chunks of the story. By identifying the similarities and differences in the visions, the group will get better acquainted with the substance of the story.

Both men received visions about what God was doing in them and in their midst. Both men received their visions during times of prayer. The regular Jewish hours of prayer were in the morning and evening—with the evening prayers occurring around 3:00 p.m. (Keener, *IVP Bible Background Commentary,* p. 330). Consequently, the narrative implies that Cornelius kept the Jewish calendar for his prayer times. Peter, likewise, was praying at the time of his vision (v. 9). Both visions instructed the men to do something, to take a specific action. Cornelius was instructed to send for Simon Peter and invite him to his home. Peter was instructed to change his whole perspective about what was considered "unclean" and not be afraid to go with the Gentile servants back to Cornelius's house. Both visions included direct communication: Cornelius conversed with an angel, while Peter heard and conversed with the Spirit of the Lord. Verse 13 describes the Spirit as a voice, but Peter responded by calling the voice, "Lord." Later, the voice was identified as the Spirit in verse 19.

Both visions left the men with unanswered questions. Cornelius had no idea what Simon Peter had to say to him. All he knew was that he was to find him and bring him back to his house for instruction. Peter was also in the dark in many respects. He had a vision about the "unclean" things, but at this point, he had no idea how that was to be understood or applied. All he knew was that he was to follow the men back to the house of Cornelius and tell them what he knew. It is clear that somewhere along the way, Peter began to understand what the vision meant, but he didn't understand directly after the vision. He was still wondering (v. 17) and thinking about it (v. 19) when Cornelius's men came to him.

There are some significant differences in the visions the men had as well. The most obvious is the complexity of Peter's vision. Cornelius encountered an angel, and the substance of the vision was an affirmation of his righteous life and his attention to the poor—along with the directive to bring back Simon Peter. The substance of Peter's vision was to realign his understanding of the "unclean" things under the law. The vision included the use of "visual aids," while there was no need for that with Cornelius. Another important distinction is that it took Peter three times of seeing the sheet with unclean animals before the vision concluded. Cornelius's vision was direct and easily understood, while Peter's was harder for him to grasp and more difficult for him to interpret.

Try to help the group stay on the question of similarities and differences. Further questions will go deeper into the meaning of the vision and the implications.

Question 5. This is a substantive question that gets at the heart of the passage's truth. Help the group first identify why the vision was so unnerving to Peter. Peter had been taught all his life that there were "unclean" animals and people. As a member of God's chosen people, he was well aware that he was never to partake of certain animals according to the law. The stipulations that came from the law about how the Israelites were to live, behave and interact with their God were the very distinctives that kept them separate from all other people groups. Even in the first century, the law was what made them different from their Roman oppressors and from the pagan cultures surrounding them. Not eating of certain animals was part of their particular religious culture.

Yet here God was challenging Peter to do the very thing that he had never done: eat unclean animals. That it was God telling him to do that would be unnerving for Peter. Try to help the group imagine what it would have been like for him to hear and see this and try to reconcile it with his understanding. Something had changed, and Peter was desperately trying to grasp what was happening.

The substance of the vision is in verse 15 when God explains a bit of the strange vision. There is, indeed, something new happening in the world. God was calling something that was previously called "impure" by a new designation: "clean." God was the one who was doing this. He was the one who, in essence, was redefining things for his people. At this point, God did not explicitly reveal that he was talking about the gospel going to the Gentile world. The vision remained in the realm of eating unclean animals.

Question 6. There were a variety of barriers being crossed for the first time in these few verses. The Gentile messengers arrived at Simon the Tanner's house in Joppa where Peter was staying. The messengers knew enough about Jewish culture not to enter the house but to call out. This act alone highlighted the barriers that existed between these peoples. Peter was still unsure about what was going on, but the men explained that their master had also had a vision and the vision included Peter coming to explain things. Peter must have been connecting the dots, because he was able, at this point, to invite a group of Gentiles into a Jewish house. Verse 23 is significant because it points out the move from *barriers* to *hospitality*. Up to this point, Gentiles had been considered "unclean," but now they've been invited into the house as guests. This was a crucial move for Peter to make. He offered hospitality to these Gentile messengers in many ways, providing table fellowship and overnight housing.

Another critical barrier was crossed when Peter arrived in Caesarea. He had been traveling with a groundbreaking group, a group of Gentiles from Caesarea and Jewish believers from Joppa. When he arrived, he entered the home of Cornelius, breaking another substantial barrier. Here was a Jewish man, who, most likely, had never set foot in a Gentile home, and he entered into the home of a Gentile, a Roman soldier. Entering his house would undoubtedly have meant having table fellowship with Gentiles and would be another barrier overcome.

Question 7. This will be a question that is difficult for people to answer honestly because it requires being vulnerable. Try to encourage the group not to remain with superficial and abstract answers but to think deeply and share honestly. There are certainly barriers that exist between ethnic groups today in many communities or between socio-economic groups. Maybe the group will identify barriers between people of certain lifestyles, such as homosexuals and heterosexuals, or between married and unmarried couples. The goal is to pinpoint walls that keep people from interacting and extending hospitality to one another.

Question 8. With the vision, the Gentile messengers and going to Cornelius's home, Peter began to understand that God was drastically changing something. Peter began to understand one of the key elements in the gospel: it is for everyone, not just for the Jews. This was a momentous epiphany for Peter and, consequently, for the fledgling church. Peter understood that what God had been trying to show him was that the people he used to see as unclean were no longer identified as such. The barrier between Gentile and Jew had been demolished. In verses 34-35, Peter grasped that God's heart is for all to know him and to come to him. This has been true since the beginning of time, but Israel did not always understand that to be true. The law that kept people separate in order to help Israel be a light to the nations had become a cultural and missional barrier. Now Peter saw clearly that Jesus had broken down any barriers, and the gospel must go out to all people.

Question 9. Encourage the group to walk through these verses and list or describe all the elements of the story that seem surprising. They are all aspects of the historical events of Jesus' life, ministry, death and resurrection, but some of the specific elements that he emphasized may seem surprising. For instance, Peter took two verses to talk about Jesus being seen by witnesses already chosen. This is important to establish the historical event of the resurrection. Peter seems to be emphasizing the fact that Jesus was actually seen by many eyewitnesses, perhaps because the Gentiles would have needed some secure evidence that Jesus had been raised from the dead. Peter also emphasized that the eyewitnesses were people who had been with him for a long time, and because they had been with him, they were qualified more than any others to recognize him in his resurrected state. Other elements that might need discussion are the statements about Jesus being the judge of the living and the dead or the connection with the prophets' messages about forgiveness of sins.

There are aspects of Peter's sermon that we might not include in a conversation today, but they were important to Peter's audience. It can be a helpful exercise to identify those elements as a way of emphasizing the need to bring the gospel to people in ways that will connect with them.

Question 10. The interruption of Peter's sermon by the Holy Spirit is equally as historic as Peter's message. Jews believed that the Spirit inspired only righteous people with divine utterances, such as the manifestation of tongues would have been categorized as. In addition to this, Jews understood from the prophets (Joel 2:28-29) that God would pour out his Spirit on his people in a future age. Thus, the pouring out of the Holy Spirit on Gentiles would have ushered in a new understanding of the church. God would not have poured out his Spirit on those he did not accept, thus this event would force the Jewish believers to accept the Gentiles as part of God's people.

Before this experience, the gospel message was mainly being preached to the Jewish world. Even though there had been disciples who had gone to Gentiles (Acts 8 with the Ethiopian eunuch), the church as a whole had not wrestled with the concept of including the Gentiles in the church. As a result of this experience, Peter shared with the church in Jerusalem and convinced them that God had done this. Acts 11 continues the story of Peter explaining his actions, and it ends with the rest of the Jerusalem believers praising God, saying, "So then, God has granted even the Gentiles repentance unto life" (Acts 11:18).

Question 11. This question is designed to connect the story of Peter to the focus of this study guide. Both Peter and Cornelius extended hospitality to people whom they previously would have avoided. This passage shows that hospitality is crossing barriers in order to reach others who are dissimilar. It is easy to be hospitable to people with whom we have no differences or no prejudices. It is quite another thing to extend protection, provision and the means of life to people across deep divides from us. Yet this is what God calls us to do as his people. Help the group discuss the actions of hospitality in this narrative and the consequences of it.

Question 12. It is crucial to help the group be specific in the application of this study. It will require group members to move out of their comfort zones and cross barriers, whether the barriers are ethnicity or lifestyle. Make a plan to check in with group members during the week or the coming weeks to see how they are doing with their application. Hospitality can break down walls in amazing ways. Encourage them to see how effective extending hospitality can be in building relationships and sharing the gospel.

Patty Pell (M.A., Old Testament Studies, Denver Seminary) is a staff worker with InterVarsity Christian Fellowship on the campus of the University of Northern Colorado and at Christ Community Church in Greeley, Colorado. She is the author of Esther *in the LifeBuilder Bible Studies series.*